$\pi = 3.14$

D1347937

THE BRAIN BOX

DAVID HODGSON
& TIM BENTON

THE ESSENTIAL GUIDE TO SUCCESS
AT SCHOOL AND COLLEGE

Independent Thinking Press

First published by
Independent Thinking Press
Crown Buildings, Bancyfelin, Carmarthen, Wales, SA33 5ND, UK
www.independentthinking press.com

Independent Thinking Press is an imprint of
Crown House Publishing Ltd.

First published 2014. Reprinted 2014, 2015, 2016.

British Library of Cataloguing-in-Publication Data

A catalogue entry for this book is available from the British Library.

Print ISBN: 9781781351130
Mobi ISBN: 9781781351666
ePub ISBN: 9781781351673
ePDF ISBN: 9781781351680

Designed and typeset by seagulls.net

Printed and bound in the UK by TJ International, Padstow, Cornwall

CONTENTS

INTRODUCTION

The rules for this book - there are no rules!

This book is yours.

That means you can do what you like with it.

There are places to make notes and to doodle.* There are things to pull out. There are quizzes and other tools that will help you get to know yourself better.

By the time you're finished with it, this book should be a mess. It will have been your companion through your exams and, like a good friend, it will have helped you get through the tough stuff.

Love this book. And make it your own.

* We tend to focus better when we're doodling, so become a doodler! You don't have to be an amazing artist – just do what comes naturally. Sooner or later, you'll start remembering what you were doing/studying just by looking at the doodles. Try it!

WHAT DO YOUR DOODLES SAY ABOUT YOU?

* **Arrows** – ambition and aggression. Book your place on the next series of *The Apprentice*.

* **Boxes** – a methodical thinker.

* **Eyes** – you feel you're being watched and judged by others. You want to be noticed. Audition for *Britain's Got Talent*.

* **Stars or flowers** – you're romantic.

* **Question marks** – you're uncertain about your future.

* **Umbrellas** – you're bored.

* **Webs** – you feel trapped.

You are creative, so go for it!

ONE OF A KIND

There are seven billion people on this planet, yet we're all unique! We have different talents and abilities. We all have something positive to offer the world.

Just take a look at the end of your thumb. There's the proof, right there! Your fingerprint is unique to you. No one else has it. No one ever will.

That makes you *different* to everyone else. But *different* in a good way.

We're all different.

There are some people who like cheese. Others hate it.

Some people love thrash metal, others indie, some just want to listen to chart stuff.

Some people love to play computer games all the time, some just like to watch TV or hang out with their friends.

It would be a boring world if we were all the same, if we all thought the same and wanted to do things in the same way.

And it's like that with revision. It's like that with learning.

How we learn can be as individual as a fingerprint.

Hopefully this book will help you to work out *your* way of doing things.

Once you've worked out the best methods, you're sorted. You can keep on learning. You'll do better, get smarter and keep growing.

Then you can make your mark on this world.

Your profile:

My fingerprint

Name: ....

Age: ....

School: ....

Revision makes me (circle the ones which apply):

excited   bored   worried   happy   miserable   vomit   wee myself   hungry

give up   energised   focused   not care   other

Relationship status (circle the ones which apply):

single   happily single   unhappily single   on the lookout   in a relationship

tried dating once but can't be bothered any more   in a relationship with my mate's girlfriend/boyfriend (don't tell them!)   I love my dog/cat/gerbil/tarantula/ferret/bearded dragon/other!

3

My idea of happiness is:

....

....

....

....

When I grow up, I want to be:

....

....

....

Got a picture of
yourself you like?
Why not stick it here:

Status right **now**:

....

....

....

....

....

RIGHT HERE, RIGHT NOW ...

Which one of these statements applies to you, right now at the start of things?
Tick the box and then read the section below that's meant for you.

- ❏ I'm massively stressed about my exams. **Read 'Stressed'**

- ❏ I'm working well right now. **Read 'Working well'**

- ❏ I want to do well so I'm reading this to find out if there's anything else I can do to improve myself. **Read 'What else?'**

- ❏ I always do well in tests so I'm not too bothered. **Read 'Not bothered'**

- ❏ I want to revise, but I don't know how. **Read 'I want to but ...'**

- ❏ Nothing works for me, I can't remember anything. **Read 'Nothing works'**

- ❏ Life's too short to revise. **Read 'Life's too short'**

- ❏ I don't care how I do. **Read 'Don't care'**

- ❏ I say I don't care how I do. But I do really. **Read 'Do care, really'**

Stressed

So you're massively stressed about your exams.

You probably have a really clear idea about where you're heading in life and know that it starts now. Maybe you feel a weight of pressure to do well, either for your parents or your teachers. Maybe you have an older sibling who excels academically and you feel you need to compete – doing as well as them or even better.

You aren't the first person to feel this stress, and you won't be the last. There are scores of other young people, up and down the country, who feel the same way. But that doesn't make your feelings any less real. What you need to do is manage your stress – you are more likely to mess up if you don't get a handle on your anxiety.

First off, you need to talk about the pressure and how it is making you feel. Talk to friends, a teacher you get on with or a parent. Maybe there is a school adviser or counsellor. Just talking about your anxieties will help.

There are bits and bobs in this book that you should read – browse the stuff about the brain (and read all the 'Inside the Brain Box' sections), particularly the bits on what stress does to you. Forewarned is forearmed! Read about motivations – do you want to do well for the right reasons (see page 62)? You might have always got good grades at school and haven't really experienced failure. However, we all fail sometimes. That's just life! We need to know how to deal with it and, more importantly, know that it isn't the end of the world. Even if you fail all your exams (and we doubt you will), you will find a way to move forward. Read what we have to say about dealing with failure (page 58) – it will help you to realise that there is *always* a way forward.

If you need specific revision tips, look at our suggestions in Chapter 4.

If panic is making you avoid revision, read our thoughts on that too (see page 106).

Also read what we have to say about time management and making sure your life is in balance (see page 137). If all you have is great exam results, you may not have all you need …

Working well

You're thinking, I'm already working well right now.

Hey! Good for you. But don't get complacent! Pace yourself. Read what we have to say about making a planner (see page 111) and keep going.

There is a danger that you're working *hard* not *smart*, so check out what we've got to say about *effective* revision (see Chapter 4). Also, if you're doing the same things all the time you might get bored, so make sure you're shaking it up from time to time. Read what we've written about keeping it fresh in Chapter 3.

What else?

You want to do well, so you're reading this to find out if there's anything else you can do to improve yourself.

Great attitude! What you've realised is that success comes in many forms. Good grades are part of this, and you'll find some brilliant tips to sharpen up your revision sessions in Chapter 4.

But it's also important to be a rounded individual. Have you considered work experience? Is your only hobby getting to the next level on *Call of Duty*? How do you spend your spare time and holidays? What are you putting out there on Facebook or Twitter? It's no good having great grades if the Internet is awash with reasons for future employers not to give you a great job! Have a look at our thoughts on this (see page 62).

Why not try out some of the suggestions for time management (see page 137)? These could help you raise your game.

Make sure, of course, that you also follow our advice for exam success in Chapter 5, because that will be a great start.

Not bothered

You always do well in tests so you're not too bothered.

Oh, so you're a clever one! Good for you! But that won't always be enough. At some point, we all realise that we need to work harder at some things than we think we do. Some of us have always done well in school, but then find GCSEs need more work than we thought. Others discover this at A level – many people come unstuck in sixth form because they got their GCSE grades with little effort. Some people reach college or university before they realise, for the first time, that they have to work hard. Others get their first job and then discover they aren't as brilliant as they always thought they were.

Why take the risk? Work hard now. No one ever looks back at school and thinks, 'I wish I'd worked less!' No one ever gets the top grades at GCSE with little work. No one achieves the top grades in their A levels without serious hard graft.

Read what we have to say about your competition (see page 64). Being good isn't enough any more. You might find this section a real wake-up call.

I want to but ...

You want to revise but don't know how.

Well, good news! You have this book! Schools are usually great at telling you that you *have* to revise and even *what* to revise, but often not how to revise. Read all our tips on revision in Chapter 4. Some will work for you, others won't. Use the ones that do and avoid the ones that don't, but don't be afraid to try things out.

Nothing works

Nothing works for you – you can't remember anything.

Ah! That's not true. You just aren't revising in the right way. Read what we have to say about finding the right way to work (see page 101).

We can all learn, but we need to find the best methods for us. Once we have the tools, we'll be unstoppable. We also need to be in the right mood (see pages 24–39).

Life's too short

You think life is too short for revision.

But if you end up doing a job you hate, things will *really* drag. If you think schoolwork is boring, wait until you see the options open to you after you've flunked out.

Read what we have to say about goal setting (see page 61) and motivation (see page 65). In the bigger scheme of things, knuckling down and revising takes up only a short period of time, but the effort will be worth it.

Don't care

You say you don't care how you do.

We're aware this may be the only bit of this book you'll read, so we've probably only got about 10 seconds to make a difference.

Start the countdown …

10. Life can be crap. But just because it might have been in the past, doesn't mean it always will be (see page 20).
9. We know you don't believe it now, but you've got more to offer than you think (see page 11).
8. Just because it *feels* hopeless, doesn't mean it is.
7. Your teachers don't hate you, so stop fighting them. People will help you. You aren't worthless, regardless of what you feel.
6. Life isn't fair, but you can make it better.
5. Someone will one day think you are amazing. That may seem hard to believe right now. Try to care about your future, because one day it will matter to you.
4. Yesterday has gone, but you still have tomorrow (see page 21). Every day is a new start.
3. The voice in your head – the one that tells you everything is a waste of time and nothing can change – it's lying!
2. The voice in your head which says all that negative stuff about you is also lying.
1. If you try, things will get better: you are smarter and more capable than you realise. Really.

We hope you decide to read some more.

Do care, really

You say you don't care how you do – but you do really.

Wow. It must be hard keeping up a front all the time, pretending you're one thing but really you're another. It's probably sapping all your energy! Chill. Relax. Be yourself.

And stop reacting badly all the time and making such a fuss! The only person you're ultimately going to hurt is yourself. Get a grip! You may be worried about what your friends think, but they may not even be in your life in five years' time. It's time to step up for you.

You know all those things you want from life? No one is going to just give them to you. You need to work for them. That starts now. Sorry if that sounds harsh, but sometimes we need a reality check.

If you're busy pretending to be something you're not, it will take its toll. If you're lashing out at people and being stroppy all the time, you're going to feel very alone. This may lead to stress. Stress and worry make a real mess of us. It is good to have a healthy body, but it is just as important to have a healthy mind. Read what we have to say about looking after your mental health (page 32).

If you really do care, do something about it!

GETTING THINGS WRONG ...
GETTING THINGS RIGHT

Most people struggle to remember names when introduced to a small group of people for the first time.

Why *is* that?

What was your name again?

First, WRONG MOOD. This is because when we're introduced we're paying attention to *ourselves* not the person we're about to meet!

We may not even make eye contact because we're worrying about how bad our new haircut looks or whether we're dressed right. Maybe we're feeling nervous for a dozen other reasons. We don't even *hear* them say their name because we're not really *listening*.

Second, WRONG TECHNIQUE. We can all remember names if we follow a few simple rules.

When we first meet someone, we should *make eye contact, smile* as we shake their hand and say, 'Hello, my name is David.'

We then raise our eyebrows (the cue for them to speak) and after they say, 'Hi, I'm Paul,' we *repeat their name out loud*: 'Hello Paul, pleased to meet you.'

As we say their name out loud, we think of something weird which will help us associate their name with something about them. A rhyming word is good – so if *Paul* is *tall* or *small* we can use the rhyme, *tall Paul tall Paul*. If he looks like a famous Paul, we could imagine him dressed like Paul McCartney. Try it – it works!

Third, WRONG PRACTICE. Practice is vital. Practice develops skill and peak performance.

If you use this technique, you'll get better at remembering names. The more you do it, the easier it will become. After a while, it will be second nature. It's great to pick up good habits, which will help you to be a more excellent version of yourself.

There are plenty more techniques in the book to try, so keep reading!

The process of learning and revising effectively is the same as remembering names effectively. We can learn and revise in this way too.

* People often don't learn well because they aren't paying attention. Their minds are somewhere else during lessons and they simply don't hear it.

* Nerves also limit us by turning our negative energy inwards, making us focus on ourselves rather than the learning (which is daft when you think about it).

* Being able to enter the right mood for learning, revising and exams is crucial *and* fairly easy, when you know how.

* We don't learn *how to learn*, but this is easy to correct. The rules of learning well in class, at home and in exams are covered in this book. Knowing the rules will save you time and effort and turbo-boost your performance!

* We need to practise the techniques described in this book to improve our skill and performance.

To simplify the process even more:

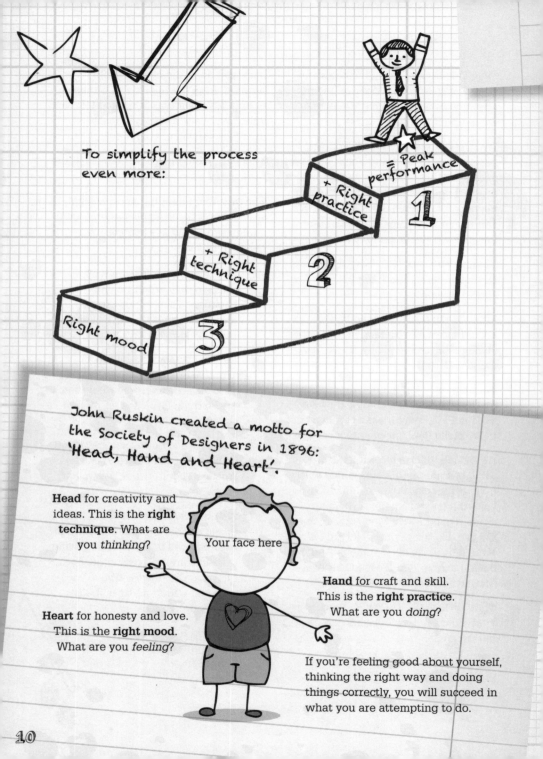

= Peak performance

+ Right practice **1**

+ Right technique **2**

Right mood **3**

John Ruskin created a motto for the Society of Designers in 1896: 'Head, Hand and Heart'.

Head for creativity and ideas. This is the **right technique**. What are you *thinking*?

Your face here

Hand for craft and skill. This is the **right practice**. What are you *doing*?

Heart for honesty and love. This is the **right mood**. What are you *feeling*?

If you're feeling good about yourself, thinking the right way and doing things correctly, you will succeed in what you are attempting to do.

CHAPTER 1

AT THE START
DEALING WITH ME!

BELIEFS

Beliefs are fascinating. They make us who we are.

Some beliefs are very useful and some are limiting.

Some strong beliefs can be permanent, whilst others are fleeting. We might once have believed in the tooth fairy or Father Christmas. We may believe we'll never be able to ride a bike. We may believe we love certain people, animals or objects.

But what are your beliefs around learning, school, education and your intelligence?

They will have a **MASSIVE** impact on your future.

What are you avoiding because you don't think you can do it?

If you believe, you can achieve, innit!
Dizzee Rascal

David says:

A teacher recently told me the mantra she shares with all of her students:

Be bigger than your problems.

The more I reflected on these five words the better they sounded.

It's so simple yet very profound. We only ever need to be just a bit bigger than the challenge before us.

When have you been bigger than a problem you faced?

Be bigger than your problems.

What used to make you scared (but doesn't any more)? What changed?

When we're young, we're scared of all sorts of things: the dark, exotic foods, buttons, wasps, Doctor Who and things that live under our bed!

As we get older, we get scared of what *might* happen.

Most of the things we are afraid of don't exist or may never happen.

The only thing we should be scared of is not living life to our full potential. Sadly, many people are too afraid to do this. Don't be one of them!

Tim says:

I was recently forced to attend a roller-disco (it's a long story). I am over 40; these things should not happen to me. My wife says, 'Come on! It will be fun. Put the boots on.' Well, I'm reasonably up for new experiences, so despite my spider-sense telling me this was a very bad idea, I put on the roller-boots. I got to my feet and wobbled forward a few steps.

'I can't do this!' I shouted to my wife, Clare.

'Yes, you can,' she said, 'just glide!'

'Glide? GLIDE? I'm on wheels!' I say. 'I want to go back!' I add.

'You can't,' Clare says. 'It's a one-way system – you have to go all the way round.'

For the next ten minutes (and it seemed like *hours*), I make my undignified passage around the edge of the room.

It was at this point that my friend, Simon – who had never roller-skated in his life and is also in his forties – speeds up and does what can only be described as a pirouette. On wheels. On flippin' wheels.

'I thought you said you'd never skated before!' I fumed.

'I haven't,' said Simon, looking far too cheerful.

'Well, how on earth are you doing it?' I asked, utterly incredulous. 'How come you aren't falling over?'

'I just assumed I could do it,' Simon explained, with a shrug. 'I've always been good at sport, and most sports come naturally to me.'

He assumed he'd be good.

This made sense. I'd put the boots on and assumed I would *not* be able to do it.

Dizzee Rascal was right: if you tell yourself you can do something, you stand far more chance of succeeding. Likewise, if you are negative and assume you won't be able to do something, the chances are you will fail.

DARE

It's a simple little word. What does it make you think about?

Truth or dare? (A great game, which normally ends with someone mooning a lorry driver!)

The song by Gorillaz?

Daredevil?

Dan Dare?

The River Dare?

Taking risks?

Bungee jumping?

Parachuting out of a plane?

Daring your mates to do something? ('Go on – I *dare* you!')

Add your own:

....

....

....

....

....

How about daring to believe in your abilities and intelligence?

Often this is something we don't dare do.

OK. Write below what you think you can get in your exams. When the results come through, what do you expect to see? Put the subject first, then the grades.

....

....

....

....

....

Have you dared to believe in yourself? Were there any grades below C? If there were, you're selling yourself short: aim higher.

Now, cross out the grades you wrote and replace them with what you would *love* to see when the results come out. Not what you think you're going to get – what you'd like to get. What would make you over the moon?

Do you think you could achieve these grades instead?

The people who get those grades are out there. They are just like you. They get those results, not because they are cleverer than you or better than you, but *because they dare to believe it's possible*, and they put the work in.

These are now your target grades. This is what you're aiming for.

Mini brain upgrade

A great belief to have is 'I am a learner.'

What have you learnt so far in life (circle the ones which apply)?

walk   talk   text   swim   play an instrument   read

write   shop   play computer games   peel a banana

which one's Ant and which one's Dec?   draw   sing   play

fall over without hurting yourself   chess   kindness   run

skip   a second language   eat   wash up   juggle

touch your nose (or elbow) with the tip of your tongue

be curious   wash up   make a bed

whistle   laugh   paint

get dressed   skateboard

drink water without choking

queue   apply make-up

join in   offer your opinion

kiss your pet   tell jokes

make friends   dance

bake a cake   smile sincerely

Add any more that you're particularly proud of.

What else do you want to learn to do?

Impossible is just a word thrown around by small men who find it easier to live in the world they've been given than explore the power they have to change it. Impossible is not a fact. It's an opinion. Impossible is not a declaration. It's a dare. Impossible is potential. Impossible is temporary. Impossible is nothing.
Muhammad Ali

ARE YOU BENDY?

Are you fixed? Or are you flexible?

Are you stuck? Or can you grow?

Are you open? Or are you closed?

I went to the gym the other day to see my personal trainer.

'Can you help me do the splits?' I asked.

'It depends,' he replied. 'How flexible are you?'

I said, 'I can do Tuesdays.'

Boom! Boom!

Some people have a fixed mindset. They say, 'I can do this' but 'I can't do that'. They don't believe they are capable of growing, of learning. They are limited by their own beliefs.

Others have a flexible mindset. They are able to grow. They say, 'I can do this' and 'I can't do that yet'. The 'yet' is important. It shows they believe that they can change. Because they think they can, they probably will.

Do you get it? If you think you can do something, you will probably do it. If you think you can't do it, you probably never will.

Whether you think you can, whether you think you can't – you're probably right!
Henry Ford

DO YOU HAVE AN OPEN OR CLOSED MINDSET?

HELLO

Find out about your mindset with this fun quiz – and get some advice at the same time. Which statements are more you? Circle A or B for each question, then tally your points at the end.

1. Challenge:
    A. I like new challenges. I enjoy the rush of pushing myself in new areas.
    B. I don't like new challenges. I prefer to stick to the things I'm good at.

2. Trouble:
    A. I tend to give up easily when things are hard.
    B. If something is difficult, I push on until I can do it.

3. Mastery:
    A. I believe that if I work hard at something, I will be able to do it.
    B. There are some things I will never be able to do, so what is the point?

4. Criticism:
    A. I don't mind when people correct my errors. I see positive feedback as a way of getting better.
    B. Why are you criticising me? Get out of my face!

5. Success:
    A. I hate seeing people do well. It makes me depressed about what I can do.
    B. I get really inspired by watching or hearing about people who do well.

6. Which motto best describes you?
    A. Don't tell me the sky's the limit when there are footsteps on the moon.
    B. If at first you don't succeed, give up.

7. How do you react to a low score or a disappointing performance?
    A. I feel like there's no point trying any more.
    B. I need to work out what I did wrong, so I can get a higher mark or better score next time.

8. You are considering chatting to someone you fancy. What is the voice in your head saying?
    A. I'd ask them out, but I think they'd turn me down.
    B. They're a bit out of my league, but I'm going to try and get them to notice me.

9. A friend suggests you listen to their favourite music but you think you won't like it. How do you respond?
    A. Yeah, I'll listen to your music.
    B. No thanks, I like what I'm listening to.

10. Which of these are you on holiday?
    A. I'm on holiday! Let's try the local food!
    B. I'm on holiday! Is there a chip shop?

1.	A = 3. B = 1.	6.	A = 3. B = 1.
2.	A = 1. B = 3.	7.	A = 1. B = 3.
3.	A = 3. B = 1.	8.	A = 1. B = 3.
4.	A = 3. B = 1.	9.	A = 3. B = 1.
5.	A = 1. B = 3.	10.	A = 3. B = 1.

Less than 12

Oh dear. You may currently have a closed mind and a glass half-empty mindset. If you open up to the possibility that you can be better, you may find the world is an exciting place and there are new experiences to be had. You will almost certainly be more happy and successful if you embrace opportunities! Get stuck in – the only one holding you back is you! You probably like the idea of being intelligent but you're convinced you aren't. If you don't believe you can get smarter, you're wrong. The good news? You can! Believe.

13-21

You're getting there. There are some key attitudes you need to address, but if you do so you'll be able to achieve so much more. Hang in there. Be more positive! If you always do what you've always done, you'll always get what you always got.

22-30

Wow! You love life. You're up for a challenge and nothing holds you back. The glass is half-full and you want the other half! Nothing's going to stop you. Well done. Keep going, superstar! You understand that your intelligence can be developed and you're happy to work at it.

So, it's important to have an open (growing) mind. The first step to succeeding is a belief that it is possible. If you don't believe you can do well, it's doubtful you ever will. If you are limiting yourself by saying things like, 'I'm thick', 'I'll never get higher than a D' or 'I'm not good at that subject', you'll seriously block your achievement.

Mini brain upgrade

Practise now by trying something new this week.

Consider it a sort of mini bucket list or attitude upgrade.

We upgrade our phone regularly and sometimes we need to upgrade our attitudes and beliefs too.

Things to try:

- A food you've never tasted.

- A book you wouldn't normally read.

- A film or TV programme you'd normally avoid.

- Talking to someone you've been meaning to for ages but haven't got round to yet.

Add some of your ideas here:

Positive people do this:

Encourage
Smile
Compliment
Say 'thank you' and 'please'
Look for the best in others
Help
Forgive
Take responsibility
Apologise
Be kind
Ignore rumours
Discuss

Negative people do this:

Mock others
Frown
Criticise
See the negative in others
Look after themselves first
Hold a grudge
Blame others
Only help others if it benefits them
Spread gossip
Argue

CHANGE THE RECORD

Try saying these out loud to your reflection in a mirror (you'll feel silly, but give it a go!):

> *I can do well.*
>
> *I can get higher grades.*
>
> *I'm clever. No, really, I am!*
>
> *If I work, I will do well.*

If you feel daft when you say these things, it is a clue that some of your beliefs about yourself are limiting you.

Sometimes we have deep-rooted beliefs about ourselves, which can go right back to when we are young.

Maybe someone told you that you aren't good at a certain subject.

Maybe someone told you that you aren't as clever as your brother or sister.

Maybe at primary school you were sat on the naughty table or the table for the children who were a bit less able than others.

These experiences shape us and, before long, we start to believe the messages we've been given.

How we see ourselves, and how others see us, really makes an impact on how we develop.

The experiences that we've had, good and bad, make us the person we are today.

Sometimes our experiences have made us smarter, stronger and more able to cope with challenges or help us to solve our problems.

Sometimes these experiences have been unhelpful.

Some of you will have been carrying around ideas about yourselves for years, and they may not be true. Just because you were seen in a particular way when you were young, doesn't mean that is how you will be forever.

Is it time for a fresh start?

Do you need to say 'Enough!' and start looking at things differently?

TAKE ACTION NOW – BE THE NEW YOU

Imagine you have a really big rucksack and you are going for a walk. You swing the bag onto your back and start walking.

As you travel, you meet people, have adventures and pick up mementos. As your journey continues, more and more things go into the rucksack and it becomes heavier and heavier.

After a while it becomes uncomfortable. Then it becomes painful. But you keep going, heaving the rucksack ever onwards and feeling more and more weighed down by it.

You feel worn out and wish you didn't have to carry the rucksack around any longer.

Eventually, you'll be so used to carrying the load that the discomfort will become familiar – like it has always been there. You will forget what it was like to be free of the burden.

It is only when the load is finally lifted off that you realise what a significant burden it was. How it had been holding you back, making you struggle and ruining your journey.

Do you feel like that? Are you weighed down by the past? If so, it's time to drop the burden!

Make choices.

Talk to someone you trust.

Decide not to live like that any more.

21

WHAT DO YOU BELIEVE?

The page opposite has been split in half. On the left side is a space for you to jot down the unhelpful beliefs about yourself that you've been carrying around for too long. It could be anything. You may not have even recognised that they were there until now.

Here are some of the many beliefs that people carry about:

I'm thick.
I can't do maths.
No one will ever fancy me.
Everyone is cleverer than me.
I'm not good enough.
Everyone hates me.

I can't write.
I can't do it.
I won't get the grades.
I'm ugly.
I can't spell.
There's no point.

I can't do anything right.
It's all my fault.
I'm a troublemaker.
I'm just an idiot.
I'm such a loser.
I don't deserve good things.

So, what are you carrying around? Write this down in the left-hand column of the page opposite.

What you would like to carry around instead?

Now, on the right-hand side, write down a better version – a new way of thinking. This is your upgrade.

Here are some examples:

✳ *I'm thick.* ⇨ *I'm good at some stuff but not everything.*

✳ *I'm ugly.* ⇨ *I have some good features and, like most people, I'm not perfect.*

✳ *I can't do maths.* ⇨ *I can do some bits of maths (e.g. fractions, percentages) but need further help on other bits (e.g. Venn diagrams, algebra).*

When you've done this, cross out what you've written on the left. That's gone. You need to stop thinking like that now. In time, those thoughts will go. It won't happen straight away, obviously, and it may take time. But keep coming back to the list on the right. Keep reading it over and saying the words to yourself – try really hard to believe it.

Sometimes the negative stuff is in us really deep. You may find you need to talk to someone else – someone you can trust – who will help you change things. Just remember: carrying the load around is painful. You'll always feel better, get further and be happier without it.

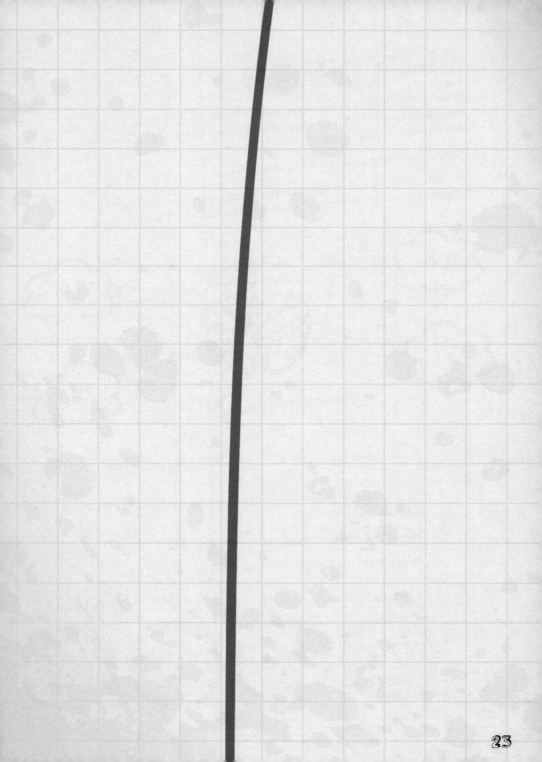

RIGHT MOODS

Whether at school or at home, we need to be in the right mood for whatever activity we're about to start. This includes sport, exercise and socialising as well as learning and revision.

There is *definitely* a best mood for learning too.

How come? Here's a clue: the brain below shows the number of ideas generated by people whilst in these different emotional states.

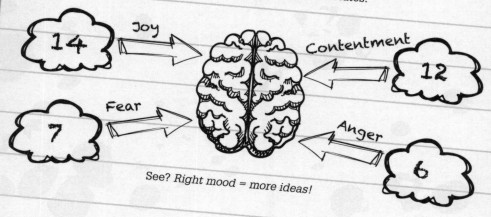

See? *Right mood = more ideas!*

As it's easier change our mood than our behaviours and beliefs, this is a sensible place to start.

We will explore four basic moods in this section.

In which of these moods do you spend most of your time?

Confuse your brain game

If we try to behave in a mood that is different to our words and actions, we can't!

✱ Try being angry while speaking in a squeaky voice and balancing on one leg.

✱ Try to watch something really funny and not laugh.

The results may surprise you. We can't mix our moods up. We can only be in one mood at a time. So, why not choose the right mood for the situation?

Goldilocks liked her porridge just right.

Not too hot and not too cold.

We can think of our learning mood in a similar way.

The task needs to be just right. Not too hard and not too easy.

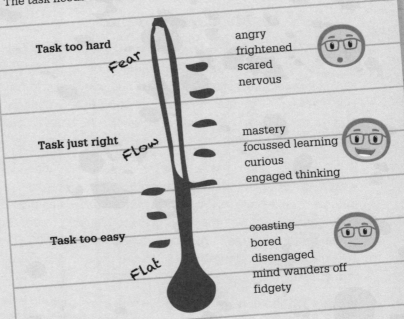

Task too hard — Fear
angry
frightened
scared
nervous

Task just right — Flow
mastery
focussed learning
curious
engaged thinking

Task too easy — Flat
coasting
bored
disengaged
mind wanders off
fidgety

Flow is when we're in the zone, at our best, unaware of time and fully engaged.

When a challenge is slightly greater than our current skill level, we're motivated to rise to the challenge. This is when we are in flow and really learning.

Flow was originally proposed by Mihaly Csikszentmihalyi as the mood of energised focus when we are fully immersed, involved and enjoying the process of an activity.

We recommend this as the ideal mood for interviews, assessments, tests and exams.

Inside the Brain Box

During *flow* and *curiosity*, the body releases beneficial hormones. Dopamine keeps us mentally alert whereas endorphins and serotonin make us feel positive and happy. Learning to *relax* increases phenethylamine (also released after eating chocolate) and oxytocin (also released when we stroke a pet or person),* both of which give our bodies time to repair and recover.

During *anger* and *nervousness* our bodies are flooded with steroids which, in the short term, put us in an alert, pumped-up, ready-for-action and on-the-edge state. Although useful initially as part of our fight, flight or fright state, this comes at a price in the long term. Usain Bolt would cause major damage to his body if he tried to run 5,000 metres at his 100-metres pace. Equally, a Mo Farah pace would not be fast enough to win shorter races.

So, go with the flow!

* When stroking someone you know well; stroking strangers may have a different effect.

Curiosity is the first stage of flow

If a class of 8-year-olds is offered a difficult challenge, they are almost all willing to have a go in front of their peers; their hands shoot into the air and they are desperate to be chosen. Me! Me! Me! Me! Me! Me!

In a group of adults, the response couldn't be more different – gazes fixed to the floor and bums shuffling nervously on seats.

Be prepared to be wrong!

Richard Branson said: 'I've learnt more from my failures than my successes.'

Learning is when we change our minds about something. We arrive at a new understanding. This is when our brain wires new connections. This is cool. This is what makes us alive. Confusion is necessary. It must be embraced as the start-point for new thinking. This is why learning has to be a bit hard! If it's easy, you can't really be learning.

Mini brain upgrade

Confusion is good. When you're stuck, write down what you're stuck on. Then thank yourself, as this is the first step to learning. Go and seek ways to unstuck yourself. Enjoy finding out. When you do understand, write that down too. You're alive (which is generally accepted as being better than the alternative)!

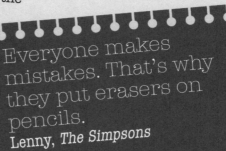

Everyone makes mistakes. That's why they put erasers on pencils.
Lenny, *The Simpsons*

Stages of learning

We all go through various stages to get the hang of doing something. Sadly, there aren't any short cuts.

* Stage 1: 'I can't do it, but I don't know that I can't do it!' Of course not, you haven't tried it yet!

* Stage 2: 'I'm doing it all wrong!' Of course you can't do it properly yet! Keep going!

* Stage 3: 'Hang on, I think I can do it!' Yep, you'll need to concentrate, but if you do, you can!

* Stage 4: 'Oh! I just did that without thinking about it!' Yes! Because you've learnt it so well, it's now second nature. Well done! You've truly learned!

Mini brain upgrade

Complete each sentence:

Learning is most enjoyable for me when
....

Things I'm good at, as a learner, include
....

My favourite question is ....

I get least out of learning when ....

The thing I'd like to change
about myself as a learner is

....

....

The most recent thing
I've learnt is

....

....

Grasshopper: Master, I am puzzled.
Master Po: That is the beginning of wisdom.
Kung Fu (TV series from the 1970s)

negative atmosphere   scared   lashing out

threats   stress   exams

criticism   FEAR   burying your head in the sand

discipline   feeling stuck

illness   tests   angry   frightened

What winds you up?   What calms you down?

Three glasses

Stress is weird. Sometimes we can cope with it and sometimes we can't. It also depends how much other stuff you're dealing with.

Imagine you're the *first glass*.

It's got some water in it but there is still loads of space. If this is you, you'll be able to cope with quite a lot of other stuff – like pressure – being heaped on you. You've got the capacity to take it.

If you're the *middle glass*, you're dealing with more. There are already additional pressures – more 'stuff' going on in your life. It isn't easy. You're not going to cope as well as the first person.

But what if you are like the *third glass*? You're already dealing with more than you should. You haven't got any more space. There's no room for extra stress. You're doing all you can to hold it together. Revision? You're just trying to get through the day.

Have a think now … which glass are you?

What can you cope with? You need to know – and if it's not much, let people know. Who can help you? Who can you talk to?

How do you currently deal with stress? If it works, keep doing what you do. If not, it could be time to try something else.

Am I in control of stress or is stress controlling me?

* When I feel agitated, do I know how to quickly calm and soothe myself?
* Can I easily let go of my anger?
* After school, do I walk in the door feeling good?
* Am I often distracted or moody?
* Am I able to recognise when others are stressed?
* Do I easily turn to friends or family members to help calm me?
* When my energy is low, do I know how to boost it?

Here a simple mnemonic to help you when you're feeling a bit overwhelmed:

Stop what you're doing.

Think about your next step.

Action your thoughts.

Reflect on whether this was the right thing to do.

When things get too tough

One in three people will experience some sort of mental health issue in their life – depression, anxiety, eating disorders, self-harming, panic attacks. It is important not to suffer in silence.

Talk to someone. If you feel there isn't anyone you can turn to, have a look at the Appendix and call one of the recommended organisations.

Exam time can be hugely stressful. Sometimes it can tip people over. Make sure you seek the right help at the right time.

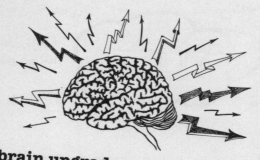

Mini brain upgrade

Stress busting idea 1

Much of what we worry about can be overcome with action.

Introduce some 'If ... then' plans to help you act more effectively.

They take this form: If X happens, then I will do Y.

This technique is particularly useful for generating good behavioural habits.

Here are some examples:

If I haven't started my homework by 6 p.m., then I will make it the first thing I do after dinner.

If I am getting too distracted by friends on Facebook, then I will stick to a five-minute chat limit and start work again for another 15 minutes.

Stress busting technique 2

Calm yourself down by gently and repeatedly passing a soft ball from one hand to the other. It is impossible not to calm down, as the activity redirects, balances and focuses our attention. This is great technique to use before an exam or test.

coasting dull fidget

FLAT

not relevant task not engaging/ interesting

bored too easy

Warning

Boredom seriously damages our ability to learn!

It's useful to recognise when we're bored – it's the first step to moving to a more resourceful mood.

Ask yourself these three questions if you think you're bored:

1. **Am I focused on the task (or distracted by other thoughts)?**
   Solution: Focus fully on one thing at a time. If you need to sort something out before attending to the current task, either do so or promise yourself you'll do it next.

2. **Is the task boring?**
   If so, make the task relevant to you. Remind yourself of the bigger picture. What is the purpose of this task? How is it helping you move towards your goals?

3. **Am I tired?**
   Sometimes boredom is not caused by a dull task. You may just be tired. If so ask yourself: why? Is it temporary due to a poor sleep last night or due to stress?

Opposite are some ways to bring a zing to a topic.

So, you're in class and you're bored by a topic. Why not try this approach which was inspired by educationalist John Davitt?

Close your eyes and randomly place your finger somewhere on this page. Approach the topic in the way suggested.

As a storyboard

As a dance

In seven words

As a radio news report

As if it was a type of car

As an animal

Only using three key numbers

As if it was a mathematical formula

As an assembly address

As a rock song

As a comic strip

As an album cover

In three words

As a 60-second play

In a text message

As a poem

In the style of a weather report

As a puppet show

As a boy band song

As a sports report

As if it were a type of shoe

As a 140 character tweet

Boredom cured? Ta daaaa!

Inside the Brain Box

By stating learning principles in a novel way, as above, the brain pays more attention. It has to process the ideas and challenge them if they contradict earlier information. Thinking about these concepts helps us to extract and remember the important points.

Remember: if you think something is crap, boring or rubbish, but others are really getting into it, it might be better to join them rather than stay flat!

How to be a rubbish learner

Avoid the right moods for learning. Instead of switching on to being relaxed, curious and to flow, stay angry, nervous and bored. Blaming others for your lack of progress is a really effective way to ensure failure. Blame your parents, teachers, peers or siblings. Or blame your environment. If you ever get stuck, use this as an opportunity to give up, accept you are useless and never try again.

Steer clear of learning how you learn best. If you don't discover how to use your brain effectively, you can avoid achieving your full potential. Be careful not to link your learning to future gains as you might accidentally motivate yourself.

Forget anything you do learn. The best way to achieve this is to avoid homework, not reread your notes or do any revision. And don't discuss your progress with others.

RELAXED

Relaxation is another mood worth mastering. And it counterbalances the three we've explored so far.

We all need to relax. Watching TV or retreating to our bedroom with our phone or laptop is often what we choose, but these are not as good for us as proper relaxation. Really relaxing involves focusing our attention and being aware of our mind and body.

Here are some easy but effective relaxation techniques which can be easily incorporated into your daily routine.

Fishy exercise

Try making your mouth into a big 'O' shape and then wrap your lips around your teeth. Whilst holding this position, alternate between making 'eeee' 'and 'oooo' sounds out loud. If you're doing this right, you should be doing a pretty good impression of a fish. This is a bit of fun and distracts us from what we were doing and thinking. We tend to carry a lot of tension in our facial muscles and this exercise removes it.

Active relaxation (30 seconds each)

* Try moving about – sitting in a chair is pretty unnatural.
* Move about to break up your revision and give yourself a natural boost.
* Stand up and balance on one leg then the other.
* Lie down and make invisible angels.
* Dance lying down.
* With one hand create a figure of eight and with the other a circle (it's very difficult to do both at the same time).
* Curl up into a ball.
* Do 20 star jumps.

You get the idea. Relax for 15 minutes a day and you'll enjoy the benefits.

Random acts of kindness

Another stress-busting technique is to do a kind deed for someone else. Researchers have discovered that random acts of kindness will make you feel better, as well as helping someone else. There are a number of websites that offer suggestions, such as www.randomactsofkindness.org and www. actionforhappiness.org.

Right, what does the average person do 55 times each day?

You should now be feeling curious as your brain searches for an answer and neurons fire in all directions looking for and evaluating potential answers. No, it's not burps, farts* or smiling!

Can you list three possible answers?

1.

2.

3.

If you had to list 20, you would probably have moved from curious to bored because the task had become a chore.

This activity illustrates how our brain likes to work. It likes to solve interesting puzzles. It likes to compare and contrast information and ideas. Build these into your work and you will learn better because you will remain curious. If we aren't given an answer, our curiosity can remain for a long time. Although it can be replaced by annoyance and frustration if we feel teased.

We learn best when we're curious. Once we have an answer, the brain usually stops thinking about the subject and moves on to something else. To keep a topic fresh and interesting make sure you keep a few questions unanswered. We also learn best when we discover answers for ourselves; so if you must know what we do 55 times each day, you'll just have to find out for yourself.

* The average person farts 17 times a day apparently.

MORE ON MOODS

Most people have a default mood setting.

Think of teachers and friends for a moment and consider their default moods, the vibe they emit.

Some people are mostly happy and positive, whilst others miserable and negative.

What is your default mood? What would your friends say is your default mood?

Mood music

Music is one of the quickest and most enjoyable ways we can change our mood.

Music affects our mind, body and spirit, so we can use it to help us access the right mood. Here are our picks for music to shift our mood.

To become relaxed	To stop being bored
Bach – Brandenburg Concertos	Up-tempo music and theme tunes to super hero and action movies
Vivaldi – *Four Seasons*	Anything people dance to
Moby – *Play*	Disco, such as Donna Summer's 'I Feel Love'
Enigma – 'Return to Innocence'	
Bellamy Brothers – 'Let Your Love Flow'	Kasabian – *Velociraptor!*
Flaming Lips – 'Do you Realize?'	Generally, music at 100-plus beats per minute will give us an energy boost.
Generally, music at 60 beats per minute will help us to relax.	

To build curiosity	To enter flow
Mozart – Piano Concertos No. 26 and No. 27	Any theme tunes to favourite childhood programmes, from *Peppa Pig* and *Postman Pat* to *Marine Boy* (from the 1960s)
Tchaikovsky – *Swan Lake*	
Robinson Crusoe Suite – TV series theme tune	Sam Sparro – 'Black and Gold'
Generally, music at around 80 beats per minute will help us to focus on the task in hand.	Generally, music at around 80 beats per minute reminds us of good times and places and will help to immerse us fully in the task at hand.

Fill in each section of the blank chart below with three pieces of music that move your mood - we appreciate our musical choices are unlikely to match yours!

To become relaxed	To stop being bored
To build curiosity	To enter flow

Tip: You can reboot your mood - just try switching it off and on again! It works for computers most of the time, and it can work for us too. If you're not in the right mood, change it!

Music quiz

Which of these statements are true?*

* Men in white vans drive faster when listening to 'Don't Stop Me Now' by Queen.
* Music can help the body heal faster following traumatic accidents.
* 'Gangnam Style' was voted the most annoying song in 2012.

* They are all true.

Inside the Brain Box

Earworms are songs we can't stop replaying inside our heads – songs like 'Who Let the Dogs Out?' and Disney's 'It's a Small World'. They deftly infect our brains and play as if on a continuous loop.

Humans have been around for far longer than written language. Music is a great system for storing and retrieving information, which is why music is present in all human cultures studied by anthropologists.

Our brain recognises repetitive beats and chords and enjoys actively predicting what will follow. Our brain feels like it is writing and orchestrating, as well as listening to music. The brain likes music.

We can apply this insight to boost our learning in three ways:

1. Use music to learn and remember information more effectively and more efficiently.

2. Use music to access a great learning mood (and avoid unhelpful moods).

3. Be active rather than passive in our learning experiences.

ZZZZZZZZZZZZZ

Sleep. We all need it.

Right now, you need about eight or nine hours a night.

How much sleep did you get this week? Write below when you went to bed and when you got up.

Sunday night	
Monday morning	_____ p.m.
Monday night	_____ a.m.
Tuesday morning	_____ p.m.
Tuesday night	_____ a.m.
Wednesday morning	_____ p.m.
Wednesday night	_____ a.m.
Thursday morning	_____ p.m.
Thursday night	_____ a.m.
Friday morning	_____ p.m.
Friday night	_____ a.m.
Saturday morning	_____ p.m.
Saturday night	_____ a.m.
Sunday morning	_____ p.m.
	_____ a.m.

Can't remember? Try filling it in this week and see where you are.

So, are you getting enough sleep?

If not, what do you need to do? Go to bed earlier, perhaps?

Write down some resolutions here:

Finding it hard to sleep?
Try some of these top ten tips:

1. No caffeine – lay off the tea, coffee, cola, energy drinks and chocolate later in the day.

2. Don't eat too late. Snacking last thing – especially on sugary stuff – will impair your sleep.

3. De-stress. Write down things you need to do or remember. This will help you to organise your thoughts – then you can say to yourself 'Tomorrow …'

4. Unplug. Xbox last thing at night is terrible for sleep. It will wire your brain and stimulate you so you're buzzing into the night. TV will excite your brain too. After 9 p.m. *switch it off!* The same is true for your mobile phone – the screen light wakes up the brain and reduces the body's ability to produce the sleep hormone melatonin. Have a full digital detox at least an hour before bedtime.

5. Breathe. Lie still. Do some deep breathing. This will calm the mind.

6. Go dark. Is your room too light? If so, wear an eye mask or ask for thicker curtains. The darker it is, the deeper you'll sleep.

7. Shhhh. Ask everybody to be quiet! And turn your phone off too! You don't need to check Facebook, Twitter, texts and so on all the time.

   'But my friend might have sent me a text!' So what? Read it later.

   'Something might have happened on Twitter.' If it did, you'll find out soon enough.

   'I need to see what's on Facebook!' Er … no, you don't.

   If you go to bed early, you won't miss out.

8. If you can't sleep, get up and do something. Don't just lie there worrying.

9. Listen to your body. Feel sleepy? You probably are! Go to bed!

10. Stick to the rhythm. Going to bed at 3 a.m. one day and 10 p.m. the next … up at 6 a.m. one day and 11 a.m. the next? Your body won't like it! Get into a good sleep habit.

Night night! Zzzzzzzzzzzz.

Coffee

41

HAVE YOU GOT FOMO?*

A lot of people have FOMO! It's why they are glued to their mobile phones.

FOMO makes us constantly connect with others through social media. We are addicted. The trouble is, we fail to concentrate on things that are *really* important. We don't get our work done.

Part of being an adult is doing the things we need to do, and avoiding the things that aren't that important.

There are three types of people:

1. Those who make things happen.

2. Those who watch things happen.

3. Those who go: 'Er ... what happened?'

SUMMARY

Tick the box if you agree:

☐ In order to do well, we need to believe the right things.

☐ We are all capable of learning and developing, but we need to believe we can learn and that we can get better.

☐ Our moods have a huge impact on our ability to learn. If we are in a positive mood, learning will be possible. But if we are in a negative mood, we will find learning much, much harder.

☐ Learning is a journey – there are various stages of learning. We don't always 'get it' straight away.

☐ If we are feeling like it's all too much, we need to talk to someone.

☐ Sleep is important.

* Fear Of Missing Out.

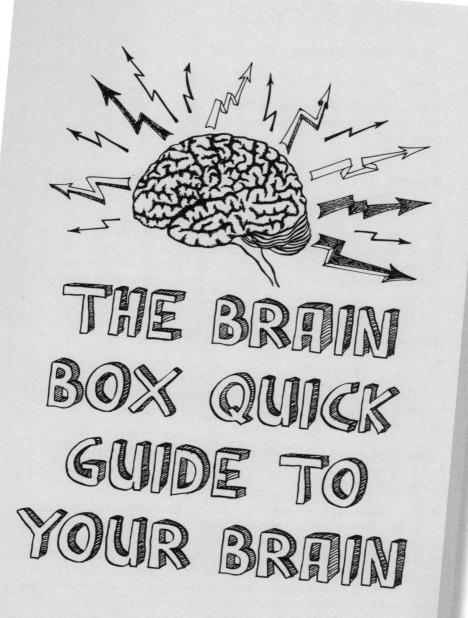

THE BRAIN BOX QUICK GUIDE TO YOUR BRAIN

BRAIN BASICS

Men have bigger brains?

☐ True   ☐ False

True. On average, men have bigger brains than women. But this does not mean that men work better, are more intelligent or more capable (sorry, lads!).

There are two hemispheres in the brain?

☐ True   ☐ False

True. You have two hemispheres. Earlier research linking one side predominantly to creativity and the other to logic has been challenged. What is clear is that approaching problems using our capacity to think with both creativity and logic is a better way to harness the enormous potential of our brain.

We only use 20% of our brain?

☐ True   ☐ False

False. We use *all* of our brain, but we use different parts for different things at different times.

The brain is 'finished' at the age of 7?

☐ True   ☐ False

False. It takes around *25 years* for your brain to finish developing. Up until then, you are still a work in progress. The last bit to develop fully is your *prefrontal cortex*. This is the bit that helps you make good decisions. Often, we need to make bad decisions before we learn the best way to do something or how to behave in certain situations. As an adolescent, you are wired to take risks and do stupid things. This is why teenagers are prone to like speed, own mopeds, play Xbox until 4 in the morning before school, snog unsuitable people, experiment with narcotics, start fights, have tantrums, get lost, act stupid, lie about where they've been and reject genuine offers of help. As we get older (in theory!), we get better at life (sadly, some people never do).

The brain is like a big dot-to-dot?

❏ True   ❏ False

Sort of. The brain is all about making *connections*. You have billions of *neurons*. These neurons connect to other neurons via *synapses*. When we learn, brain chemicals cause the synapses to fire up and wire together. The synapses have axons between them and these link the neurons. As we go over things, white matter (called *myelin*) forms on the axons and makes the connections stronger. The stronger the connection, the better we can do or know something.

It's like walking in a cornfield. The first time you walk through it, you'll make a dent but the crop will spring back up if you don't walk through it again. If you go back, the plants won't spring up quite so well. The next time, they'll get a bit more flattened. The next time, you'll be able to see where you passed before. Go through the field enough times and the path will be really well established. Memory works in the same way.

The brain produces chemicals?

❏ True   ❏ False

True. What makes the synapses fire up and wire together? Dopamine! Dopamine is the brain chemical that makes it all work.

Is Dopamine why my friend is addicted to Call of Duty?

❏ True   ❏ False

True. When you are playing the Xbox, you get a huge rush of dopamine, because it is produced by *reward* and the *anticipation of reward*. In other words, if you are enjoying yourself, or about to enjoy yourself (not like that – stop sniggering at the back!), you produce dopamine. That's why computer games are addictive.

> It certainly seems very plausible that playing video games for half a day a week may well actually structurally change the brain.
> Dr Luke Clark, neuroscientist, University of Cambridge

But dopamine isn't all bad – in fact, it can be your best friend.

Here's why. You produce dopamine under the following conditions:

RING!*

Relevance – if you see the point of something, and get something from it, you will produce dopamine. Yes, that happens with computer games, but it can happen with schoolwork too. If you keep telling yourself that what you're learning will help you get good grades, achieve your goals and be more successful, you'll click with it far easier. How does this link to other things you're learning? The more you get it, the more you'll enjoy it; the more you enjoy it, the more you'll learn.

Interesting – new or different! We all remember our first time doing something. When you are about 28 and get your first kiss (!), you'll remember it always. If you find it interesting, you'll learn it. If it isn't interesting – make it interesting.

Naughty – because when we break the rules, it becomes more interesting! Did you know that the French word for seal is phoque! Yes, it's good to have a *phoque* in water. That's naughty – but you'll remember it!

Giggle – there is a massive link between laughter and learning. That's why you shouldn't work alone.

Two important principles

1. **As we get older, the synapses we don't use wither away.**
   So, if you play a musical instrument, but give it up in your early teens, you'll find it really hard (although not impossible) to relearn it as an adult because your brain has pruned away those synapses. Did you know that a 7-year-old has 40% more synapses than an adult? That's because a 7-year-old has loads and loads of potential! They haven't started saying 'I can't' yet. If you don't use it, you lose it.

* With thanks to Roy Leighton for RING.

2. **The brain is capable of making billions and billions of connections.**
   You won't be able to live long enough but, theoretically, your brain
   has so many neurons that it is capable of making more connections
   than there are atoms in the universe! WHAT?! You have unbelievable
   potential – and your brain is *still* developing! So, when you learn
   stuff, your brain makes connections. If you go over it, the connections
   get thicker and you remember it better. If you learn in a variety of
   different ways, you make even more connections, thereby helping you
   remember more.

An example:

When you learn about something in class, you will make connections.
   If you look at the work again at home, those connections will strengthen
(the myelin gets thicker).
   If you then read more about it, you'll make more connections and reinforce
the existing ones.
   You then discover there is a TV programme about this subject on BBC
Four tonight, so you watch it. Wow! Even more connections.
   You then do some web research on it. You find some pictures and tweet
what you've learnt to some friends who are studying the same subject.
   You then get some paper and mind map everything you now know about
this subject.
   The next day, you talk to your mate about all that you've learnt and
answer their questions about it.
   The following evening, you look at your mind map again and try to draw
it from memory. You don't remember all of it, but most of it is there. You put
the original mind map beside it. You see what you've missed out.
   A few days later, you do the same thing again. This time you've
remembered more.
   A week later, you do it again.
   Your teacher gives you a test a fortnight later. You get top marks.
   When you come to revise for your exam, you're amazed at how much you
remember.
   It's close to the exam season and everyone else has to do loads of revision.
But you don't need to do as much because you've learnt it as you've gone
along. You are becoming an expert.
   Well, that's the best way to revise.

Key points

* You can 'grow' your brain with experiences and learning.

* You aren't finished yet.

* Dopamine is your friend. RING it in – Relevant, Interesting, Naughty and a Giggle!

* If you keep persisting with skills, practising abilities, learning new things and maintaining a thirst for bettering yourself, you'll be smarter as an adult.

* The less you do, the less you can do.

You will only learn if you emotionally connect with the experience.

In other words, if your heart isn't engaged, your brain won't learn.

If you want to learn, make the experience memorable, emotional or unforgettable.

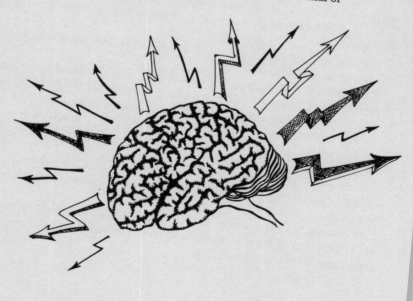

CHAPTER 2

LIFE
DEALING WITH THE WORLD AND FINDING MY PLACE IN IT

YOU

There are three questions you need to ask yourself about your life:

1. Who do I think I am?

2. Who do other people think I am?

3. Who am I really?

Learning is not just an essential part of school; it is also an essential part of life.

Learning is about being adaptable, resourceful and embracing change. Being open to and able to learn is the only skill we need.

Where can we learn?

* *Internet* – and not just Wikipedia! Look at a number of different websites. Are they all saying the same thing or is there a lot of divided opinion? Read as much as you feel you can and work out what you believe to be correct.

* *YouTube* – it's not just videos of cats falling off things!

* Read *newspapers* daily – there's bound to be something about a subject you're studying.

* Ditto *magazines* – read *The Economist*, *TIME* magazine, *National Geographic*, *Private Eye* and publications relating to your subjects. A broad general knowledge is good!

* Discover the *library*. It has books – not ebooks, not Facebook – actual books! Not sure what a book is? Ask your gran.

* Look in the *TV guide* and check channels you don't normally watch. Are there any programmes that explore what you're learning about? Tune in.

* Ask the *Oracle*! In ancient Greece, the Oracle was consulted for great wisdom! These days, your teachers are the Oracle. Ask them for advice.

* Doing MFL? Try watching subtitled *films*.

Your work is going to fill a large part of your life, and the only way to be truly satisfied is to do what you believe is great work. And the only way to do great work is to love what you do. If you haven't found it yet, keep looking. Don't settle. As with all matters of the heart, you'll know when you find it. And, like any great relationship, it just gets better and better as the years roll on. So keep looking until you find it. Don't settle.

Steve Jobs

※ When did you last visit a *museum*? You'll be amazed at how much stuff you can learn – not least the enormous cost of a bendy pencil bearing the museum logo!

Success and happiness come from us making the most of our own talents and abilities. Being the best we can be. Not trying to be somebody we're not. Comparing ourselves to others is corrosive. Life is our major work of art.

Psychologist Gary Reker has identified the principal features of happy people. How many of these do you practice?

☐ **Action**: I socialise as part of groups, clubs or societies.

☐ **Meaning**: I do what I enjoy and enjoy what I do, focusing less on status and money.

☐ **Organisation**: I plan and organise my time and goals.

☐ **Worry less**: I realise most worries never come true and focus on what I can do to improve situations rather than feeling swept along by events.

☐ **Authenticity**: I learn to be happy with who I am. I don't worry what others think of me. I like myself.

☐ **Positivity**: I choose to think optimistically. I focus on the present, not regretting the past or fearing the future.

> We are all born originals – why is it so many of us die copies?
> Edward Young

Inside the Brain Box: avalanche!

Little changes can make a big difference. The pressure group 38 Degrees takes its name from the critical angle at which human-triggered avalanches are most frequent. One degree below, the snow is benign and won't fall. But an extra one degree can make a huge difference.

Just adopting one idea from this book could help you dramatically, though you may need to try out a few before you find the right one for you.

Ideas for small improvements I can make:

....

....

....

....

....

....

....

....

....

....

....

....

....

MOTIVATION

You are always motivated to do your best? Yes ☐ No ☐ Maybe ☐

The best motivation comes from within.

Research shows that when we're motivated externally, especially with threats or punishments, the results are worse. Even treats from parents are not the best incentive. Carrots and sticks are not the best motivators. Sometimes we need to look inside for motivation.

We've asked many teenagers how they motivate themselves at school. We've noticed some interesting patterns in their answers.

First, imagine you're an amoeba. You live in water and absorb everything you need from the water around you. No need for fancy restaurants, expensive beauty products, shiny flushing toilets or Internet dating.

Essentially you only have two moves: you either move towards stuff you like, such as food, or you move away from stuff you don't like, such as toxic chemicals or hungry, bigger creatures (which is most of them).

As humans, we either move towards stuff we like or away from stuff we don't like.

This mostly happens in our heads so quickly that we don't even realise we're doing it.

Teenagers who do well at school, and who are strongly motivated, tend to have one 'move away from this' scenario, like a YouTube-style clip, which they replay in their head, and two 'I'd like to move toward that' scenarios, which are again like video clips.

The clips involve pictures (the movie scene), words (usually self-talk) and feelings (positive feelings in 'toward' clips and negative feelings in 'away from' clips).

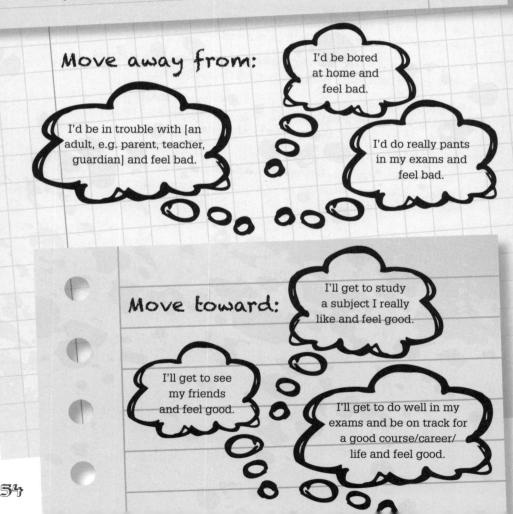

So, what do you think about when you think about school? What clips do you run in your head when you wake up and contemplate the day ahead of you?

Whatever it is, this is your current motivation.

Is it strong enough? Does it feature 'away from' and 'toward'?

If it only features 'away from', you probably won't enjoy school. You'll only feel bad when you're there.

If you have some 'toward', you'll feel good when you get to school. The most motivated teenagers tend to have the socialising/meet up with friends clip, so they feel happy before and between lessons, and a clip that links working hard at school with the outcome of future satisfaction. This is effective because it includes enjoying school day to day and includes a longer-term gain.

QUICK CHALLENGE: WHO WANTS TO BE A LIFE MILLIONAIRE?

Use the three lifelines from the popular TV show for the question: What do you think I should do with my life?

The three things are:

1. **Phone a friend** – let them know what you're going to do. Listen to their advice. Give them 30 seconds to answer as in the TV programme.

2. **Ask the audience** – ask everyone you meet in a day that you know or ask a group you belong to, such as your football team, chess club or Zumba class. You can do this online with a Facebook friends group or equivalent.

3. **50:50** – identify your top two choices from the 'phone a friend' and 'ask the audience' research and toss a coin to decide – heads is option 1 or tails is option 2. When it lands, if your initial reaction is joy then your gut reaction is telling you this is the correct option. If it lands and your first reaction is disappointment, your gut reaction is telling you this is the wrong option. If you don't get a strong reaction, then neither option is probably the right one for you.

Have you ever wondered what it would be like to meet your future self? Most of us have.

Would it be like the film *17 Again*, where a young Matthew Perry actually looks like Zac Efron?

What will you be like when you're 25, 35, 75?

Most people say that if you want to see what you'll be like in 20 or 30 years' time, you just need to look at your parents. This thought may frighten you or thrill you with pride and limitless joy! When we work with adults in their forties, we often ask, 'If you could go back in time, what advice would you give to your 17-year-old self?'

As you can't go forward in time, just to come back again with the advice and wisdom you will gather over the next 20 years, the best we can offer is sharing the answers given by older people. Bronnie Ware, a former palliative care nurse, suggests there are two pieces of advice people tend to offer as they approach their final days. Before you read them, what do you think the advice will be?

1. **I wish I'd had the courage to live a life true to myself, not the life others expected of me.** This was the most common regret. When people realise that their life is almost over, and look back, it is easy to see how many dreams have gone unfulfilled. Most people attempt less than half of their ambitions. It's OK to want to please those around us, but be careful that it's not at the expense of yourself. From the moment we lose our health, it is too late. Health brings a freedom very few appreciate until they no longer have it.

2. **I wish I'd let myself be happier.** Until they are close to death, many people do not realise that happiness is a choice. They have remained stuck in old patterns and habits. The perceived 'comfort' of familiarity has stifled their emotions and lives. Fear of change had them pretending to others, and to themselves, that they were content – when deep inside they longed to laugh properly and have silliness in their life. When you are on your deathbed, what others think of you is a long way from your mind. How wonderful to be able to let go and smile again, long before you are confronting death. Life is a choice. It is *your* life. Choose consciously, choose wisely and choose honestly.

Mini brain upgrade:
10 questions to ponder

1. What have you desired, only to be disappointed once you owned it (e.g. clothes, games)?

   ....

2. What have you learnt by observing others?

   ....

3. What is the best advice you've given to someone else? Did they take it?

   ....

4. Why are people judged by how they look?

   ....

5. Ask someone how they remember an event you both attended and compare their interpretation to yours. How do they differ?

   ....

6. What do you daydream about?

   ....

7. What is your greatest fear?

   ....

8. When have you spread a good mood around?

   ....

9. How have you changed as you've got older?

   ....

10. What cause, if any, would you die for?

   ....

WELCOME TO YOUR FUTURE ...

There are two things that contribute to our future: our past and our present.

The past

The negative events from our past should not shape our future. Sometimes it's good to draw a line and say, 'Enough! I've had enough of people saying bad things. I've had enough of believing this about myself. From now on it's going to be different.'

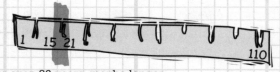

Right now you're probably somewhere between 15 and 21. Statistically, you probably have around 60 more years ahead of you. Some of you 70 or even 80 years, maybe longer.

Wow! That's a long time.

At 16, the following is true:

- ✳ Most of your life is ahead of you.

- ✳ You are still developing.

- ✳ Your hormones are doing many strange things to your body.

- ✳ You are not yet an adult.

- ✳ Your parents are annoying.

You can't really blame yourself for the things that have happened so far. Part of growing up is about making mistakes and failing. That's OK. We can learn from the past.

Sometimes things go wrong. We mess up. It is how you deal with it that is important. Do you give up? Do you have a tantrum? Do you say 'I can't do it' or 'I'm thick'?

No! You chalk it up to experience and move forward.

Can you learn from failure? Yes!

Could you have done anything differently to get a better result? Probably.

We're not defined by our failures, but how we deal with our failures defines us.

Famous failures

* Einstein didn't speak until he was 4 years old. His teachers said he would never amount to much.

* Walt Disney was fired from a newspaper for lacking imagination and ideas.

* Steve Jobs was fired from the company he started!

* A record label rejected The Beatles because they didn't think the band had a future in show business.

* Stephenie Meyer sent her *Twilight* saga to 15 publishers – 14 rejected her!

* J. K. Rowling had her Harry Potter books rejected by 12 publishers. Within five years, she went from living on benefits to being one of the richest women in the world.

* Michael Jordan was dropped from his school basketball team.

* Eminem dropped out of school and struggled with drugs and poverty.

* Elvis Presley was fired after a gig and told he should get a job driving a truck.

* Several film companies rejected *Star Wars* before 20th Century Fox accepted it. It has gone on to be one of the most successful franchises of all time.

Our present

Assuming the past isn't holding us back, the key to a better future is thinking about the here and now. The decisions we make now will have a huge effect on our future.

* Should I go out with him/her?

* Should I give up piano lessons?

* Should I get in that car if I know the driver has been drinking?

* Should I revise or go out?

* Should I go to bed or play Xbox?

* Should I tell someone I'm unhappy?

It's good to think hard about the decisions we make.

How long do we live?

There isn't a simple answer. Here are some possible answers.

* The average UK life expectancy is 80, but most people live into their seventies, eighties or nineties.

* It depends where you live (e.g. life expectancy in Afghanistan is 44).

* It depends on whether you are male or female.

* How long is a piece of string?

* Until your number is up.

* As long as you want to.

* Forever.

It depends on your lifestyle too. Until you are married!

How long do you think these organisms live for? Can you match them up?*

In reality, we live for a moment. Blink and we're gone.

And our lives are made up of thousands of moments. Each moment can be used for good or bad. Each moment never comes again.

The time between *now* and *your exams* comprises of a very few moments, in the scheme of your life. Right now, it might seem as if it is too much effort to work. It is more enjoyable to play than revise. You want to live each moment for pleasure and fun.

Tortoise	40 years
Baobab tree	140 years
Fly	14 years
Dog	48 years
Camel	10 years
Elephant	2,000 years
Swan	58 years
Bacteria	2 weeks
Goldfish	Forever

But, if you *do* choose to work in these moments, the moments in the future may be easier.

* Answers: tortoise – 140 years; baobab tree – 2,000 years, fly – 2 weeks, dog – 14 years, camel – 40 years, elephant – 58 years, swan – 48 years, bacteria – forever, goldfish – 10 years.

If you think school is boring, wait until you have to do a job you hate! That will be really boring. If you do the right thing with these imminent moments, you will have more choice later on.

Your exam grades are not the *most* important thing in your life. But they are important. They will give you more choice in the future.

Right now: choose wisely.

> You must choose, but choose wisely.
> The Knight Templar, Indiana Jones and the Last Crusade

GOALS

We all need something to aim for. If we haven't got a goal, we'll just drift. The most successful people have goals.

Tick the box if you hope to achieve the following before leaving school:

❑ Good grades

❑ A skill

❑ An ambition fulfilled

❑ Get together with that boy/girl that you've fancied since Year 7?

Or add some of your own

❑ ....

❑ ....

❑ ....

If you know what you're aiming for, you're more likely to get there. Imagine playing football without any goals. What would be the point?

Whose goals are you working towards?

Often we meet young people who say they want to be a doctor or a lawyer or an engineer. These are great ambitions, if they are *yours*.

But sometimes we choose career paths because it's what is expected of us.

My parents were both doctors, so I will be too.

All my brothers have gone to university, so I need to go too.

If I don't do well, I will be a disappointment to my parents.

If you pursue a dream that isn't your dream, you may end up unhappy. Make sure you are doing it for the right reasons.

We can spend our lives trying to please others. It's good to be kind and help other people, but sometimes we need to make decisions for our own good, not just to keep other people happy.

It may take bravery, but that's good too.

Are your ambitions too low?

Sometimes people expect too little from life. They get stuck in a rut or they don't believe there is anything good to do out there.

People who don't work hard in school often say things like, 'What's the point?'

Have you given up because you don't see the point?

We are exposed to a relentless stream of information. We have mass communication and can blog, tweet, upload, download, watch and share like never before.

But are we using our ability to communicate wisely?

Imagine if someone from the 1920s arrived here in the present day. They get chatting to you and you show them your mobile phone.

I say! What an enchanting device! Does it run on steam?

No, but it is an amazing tool. I can access all the information in the world from here and can learn about everything that has ever happened. I can check facts, discover information, learn about what is happening across the planet, communicate with millions of people around the world and hear what they have to say. I can do all that and more from this little thing that I keep here in my pocket.

Bless my soul! That's incredible! I can scarcely believe my eyes! But what do *you* do with it? How do *you* use this great wisdom?

Well, mostly I just look at videos of cats falling over and pick fights with strangers.

Software is getting better at harvesting information from social media too. Future employers will love to know all about you from your online profile.

Is Facebook full of pictures of you on drunken nights out? Does your Twitter account mostly feature nonsense and tweets about how bored you are in class?

If someone could access all this information about you (and they will), what will it say about you?

Your online presence is becoming more important than your CV when it comes to jobs. How is your reputation? Think before you upload.

Remember: nothing you post on the Internet is truly private. Someone somewhere will be able to find it and make it public.

WARNING

WE HAVE A CYBER-FOOTPRINT — EVERYTHING WE WRITE, UPLOAD, TWEET, SHARE AND COMMENT ON IS OUT THERE ...

FOREVER

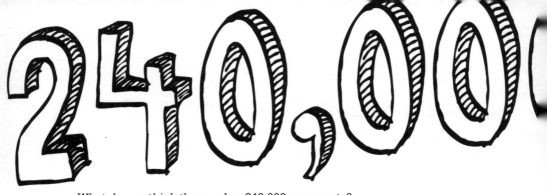

240,000

What do you think the number 240,000 represents?

It's the number of young people graduating each year from UK universities with a first class or 2:1 honours degree. This is a big number. Succeeding in life is not only about success in exams; we need to do our best in *everything* we do (including exams). Growing a positive mindset underpins this goal.

What is your competition?

There are people out there who are hungry and motivated.

They are not afraid to work hard.

They want the best jobs and nothing is going to stop them.

They might be in your class.

They might live across the world.

There are people who do *four* hours of homework a night.

There are people who do *none*.

Who is more likely to do well?

There are people who get a job whilst they are still at school.

There are people who run their own businesses alongside their studies.

There are people who arrange work experience in the school holidays to give them the edge over other young people.

There are people who undertake a wide range of extracurricular activities because they know this will make them more appealing to universities and employers.

It is a competitive world.

Are you doing enough?

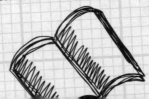

Tim says:

I was recently working on interview skills with some Year 13s. Two girls in the class wanted to study marine biology at university. I asked one girl what she had done over the holiday to improve her chances of getting on to the course. 'Er ... nothing,' she replied.

I asked the other girl the same question. She had spent the summer working for free on a marine project in Cornwall.

One got a place on her preferred course, the other got rejected. It won't take a genius to work out which one was which.

Steps

What do you ultimately want to do? It's important to know what skills you need to get you to where you want to go.

Here are two examples:

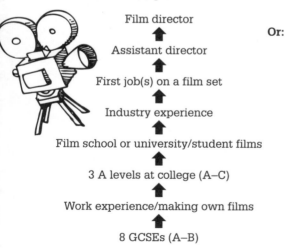

Film director

Or:

Mechanic
↑
Apprentice
↑
College/work experience
↑
5 GCSEs (A–C)

Film director
↑
Assistant director
↑
First job(s) on a film set
↑
Industry experience
↑
Film school or university/student films
↑
3 A levels at college (A–C)
↑
Work experience/making own films
↑
8 GCSEs (A–B)

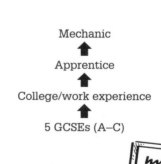

If you don't get *your* grades, how will it affect *your* plans?

YOUR LIFELINE

In the bottom left-hand corner of the page opposite is a small circle that represents you today. You may like to draw a smiley face in it and write today's date.

The circle in the top-right corner represents you in the future. Again draw a smiley face and add a date – this should be between two and five years into the future (research suggests these are optimal time frames).

Next, identify a goal that is really important to you – for example, a certain job, college place or lifestyle. (Hint: It has to be your dream. Don't put in something that you have no real control over, like winning the lottery or your football team winning trophies.) Write this in or next to the circle at the top of the page.

Now, draw in some milestones between the two circles. These are things you will need to achieve to reach the goal at the top of the page. Above the line, include the positive and proactive stuff that will move you towards your goal, and below the line, the stuff you need to avoid doing to reach your goal (this often includes procrastination).

Pull out this page and pin it up somewhere prominent.

If route A fails, always have a plan B!

If you work hard now, what benefits are there for you in the future?

For you, what is the point of achieving the best grades you can? A place on a great course? The next step to your ideal job?

It needs to be something BIG and WOW to keep you revising.

So, why are you revising? What do you want to do next?

stuff I can do more of for more success

1/4/19

Work abroad

My degree

Stuff to avoid for more success

work hard

work experience solicitor + CAB.

University of Warwick

great 'A' Levels

read + apply BRAINBOX

avoid distractions

Me YR 11
1/4/14

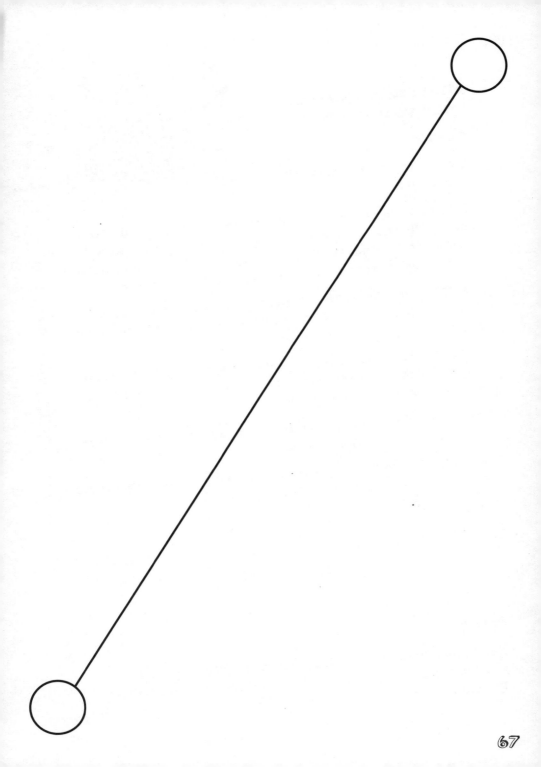

Mini brain upgrade: mind your future

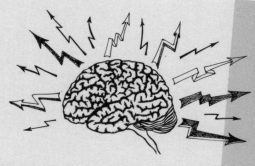

Part 1

Imagine you have finished all your exams.

It is months later – results day. You are standing by your front door holding the envelope that will soon reveal your grades. Imagine the feelings swirling around your body. Tension, anxiety, excitement, horror – they are all competing for supremacy!

You focus on your breathing – deeper, more deliberate breaths. You open the brown envelope from the back and hear the tear of paper.

You unfold the sheet of paper inside and see that you've crashed. Your worst fears are there in front of you. All of the grades are the lowest you could have expected.

How do you feel now as you recheck and see the grades really are as bad as you thought they were?

Now finish this sentence (write down your thoughts as they occur to you – don't edit yourself yet):

If only I'd ...

....

....

Part 2

Now take a short break. Distract yourself. See if you can lick your own elbow – if you can you're in the 1% of the population who can!

Part 3

Now imagine yourself again, about to open the letter containing your results. (Oiy! Stop licking your elbow!) This time, visualise yourself standing somewhere else, such as the kitchen or your bedroom. Now feel the churning of excitement and nerves. Open the letter, and this time see the results you're aiming for. Yes! You've done it! Brilliant! The results exceed your expectations. Notice how you feel – proud, tearful, excited.

Now finish this sentence (as before, write down your thoughts as they occur to you – don't edit yourself yet):

I achieved these results because I ....

....

....

Part 4

Compare the two responses. This advice, from deep within your psyche, can help to generate ideas for moving forward. Deep down, we know our own mind and you have tapped into it during this activity. It is good to get advice from others too but, ultimately, you are responsible for your own destiny!

Part 5

On a large sheet of paper, write down what you need to do to avoid failure on the left-hand side, and what you need to do to ensure success on the right-hand side. You may need to rephrase your words from Parts 1 and 3 but don't fiddle too much. The original phrases are usually best. Pin this sheet up on your bedroom wall, the fridge door or cover of your planner – somewhere you will see it regularly. This is a great reminder to keep you on course.

OK, now you can try licking your elbow again ...

Short-term vs. long-term gain

Scientists can dream up some pretty mean experiments. In one, they offered 4-year-olds the chance to have one marshmallow now or three later, but only if they could wait for five minutes whilst sitting next to the marshmallow in an empty room. As you can imagine, the little angels couldn't resist and usually gave in to temptation. They ate the one now, rather than waiting for the three!

Similar experiments have been tried with adults producing identical results. For example, if asked whether they would prefer £100 now or £200 in one month's time, most adults opt for the £100 now.

This tells us something interesting about motivation. Short-term gain is a stronger pull than a long-term benefit. When revising, this means you could offer yourself small treats for completing a set amount of work.

Ultimately, however, we're at school for long-term rather than short-term gains.

What top three long-term gains do you hope to achieve from doing your best?

1. ....

2. ....

3. ....

Something to think about ...

✳ Xbox now or work and get good grades later?

✳ Don't revise now or get into college/university later?

✳ Revise for 15 minutes a day now or need to do four hours a day later?

✳ Have a laugh with your mates in class now or need to catch up after school?

✳ Go to the shop during free study period or have more free time in the evening?

DO YOU LOVE FILMS?

Most of us love watching films. What are your favourite genres? Action? Comedy? Adventure? Horror? Sci-fi? Romcom?

Well, no matter what sort of films you like, we bet you loved the *Toy Story* films? Come on! Admit it – you did!

They're great films *and* we can learn some really important life lessons from *Toy Story*. No, seriously!

Take *Toy Story 3*, for example. If you don't know it, the premise is basically this: Andy is going to college and needs to sort out all of his old things. There is a big misunderstanding and instead of being put in the safety of Andy's loft, Woody, Buzz and all the other toys end up being sent to a children's day centre.

At first it seems like toy heaven, but soon it becomes clear that this is nothing more than a prisoner of war camp run by an evil pink teddy bear and a one-eyed doll.

At one point, Woody is planning on making his escape, and he talks to an old toy, who has been there a long time and understands how things work. He explains that there is an evil monkey who sits in front of a bank of monitors and watches everything. If toys try to escape, he sees them and calls for back-up. No one gets out. It's like *The Shawshank Redemption*. But with toys.

The wise old toy tells Woody that his real problem is the monkey, who sees everything that goes on in the classrooms and the playground. Woody can unlock the doors or scale the walls, but has no chance of escape if he can't get rid of the monkey.

Ever feel like that? That there are things you want to do – succeed, pass your exams, get good grades – but there is always something that stops you?

We all have things that keep us from fulfilling our potential – these are our monkeys.

So what are your monkeys?

- ☐ Facebook
- ☐ Xbox
- ☐ Friends
- ☐ Music
- ☐ TV
- ☐ A job
- ☐ Family commitments
- ☐ Football practice
- ☐ Dance or drama group
- ☐ Behaviour in class
- ☐ Laziness
- ☐ Lack of motivation
- ☐ Time wasting

Write your monkeys here:

....

....

Often the monkeys aren't bad things – in fact, they're frequently good things (but not always!) that we enjoy. It's about whether they have *become* a bad thing.

For example:

✳ Friends are great, but *not* if they stop you working.

✳ Xbox is fun, but *not* if you play it until 3 a.m. on a school night.

✳ Football practice is important, but *not* if it stops you doing any school work.

Do you get the idea?

If you want to get out of here … get rid of the monkey!

So what can we do?

✳ Turn off your phone. (No, really – it does have an off button!)

✳ Give mum your Xbox lead. (Noooooooooo! Er … yes.)

✳ Sit next to someone in class who won't distract you.

✳ Cut down on extra-curricular stuff, just until the exams are over.

✳ Go to bed earlier.

✳ Get rid of your Angry Birds app.

It might take a lot of maturity or even self-discipline to do this, but if you want to succeed you need to make some good choices.

Write down some strategies here:

....

....

....

....

> Discipline is not what you do to yourself, but what you do for yourself!
> Jim Roberson

Inside the Brain Box

Researcher Richard Wiseman has identified three simple techniques to boost motivation. Try out these techniques for yourself:

1. Tell other people about your goals.

2. Reward yourself with treats when you make progress.

3. Record your progress in a journal or on a chart.

BECKY'S STORY*

Becky was at school in Birmingham. She was doing GCSE French and was entered for foundation level. Becky was predicted an E grade. Oh dear.

One day, Becky decided she wanted to do better in French, so she went to her French teacher and asked if she could attend the extra classes she knew her teacher ran after school.

'Ooh,' said her teacher, 'they're actually for the higher tier students. You might struggle a bit.'

So Becky went away, a little deflated. Her teacher thought about Becky and started to feel bad about her negative response. So she tracked her down the next day:

'Look Becky, I feel dreadful about what I said yesterday. Of course you can come along. You might find it a bit tricky, but why don't you see how you get on?'

'Yes, Miss,' said Becky, 'I will.'

Becky became one of the most regular attendees at the after-school class.

After a while, her teacher decided to enter her for higher level French. Becky wasn't likely to get it – she was still predicted an E – but her teacher thought it might encourage her.

It did. When August came and the results were out, guess what Becky got?

Yep. An A. Predicted an E, but with a bit of work and some self-belief, she turned it into an A.

If Becky can do it, so can you.

* The name has been changed but the story is true.

> You're never a loser until you quit trying.
> Anonymous

Looking onwards, outwards and inwards can help us

* **Onwards**: Stickability – keep going, even when it's tough.

* **Outwards**: Community – who is near us who can offer us help and support?

* **Inwards**: Self-regulation – have I found my motivation? Am I making good choices?

SUMMARY

Tick the box if you agree:

☐ The world is competitive and we need to be the best we can be.

☐ We all have unique talents and abilities that can be developed.

☐ We need to find inner motivation to keep us going when we don't feel like it.

☐ We all need goals – things to aim for. If we don't know where we're going, how will we get there?

☐ Life is short, so we need to make the most of it. The time you spend revising is really very small in comparison to the rest of your life.

☐ There are things that can hold us back. We need to identify these and then tackle them.

CHAPTER 3

AT SCHOOL AND COLLEGE

DEALING WITH OTHERS AND FINDING THE BEST WAY TO WORK

THE RIGHT TECHNIQUES

In this chapter we will look at some techniques that suit everyone and some that just suit us. Why? Because we're all different!

We all learn best when:
- We can work things out for ourselves.
- Learning experiences are emotionally engaging (dramatic, unusual and use all our senses).
- We feel safe and positive.
- We can choose how we learn.

We all learn worst when:
- We're spoon-fed the answers, given hand-outs and revision sheets.
- Learning experiences are dull and routine.
- We feel unsafe and will be criticised for mistakes.
- We have no control over how we learn.

There are two sorts of learning that we need to master if we are going to shine at school or college:

1. **Knowledge or 'knowing stuff'.** This means facts, pieces of information, formulae and ideas – like bricks piled high in a merchant's yard! Examples include times tables and dates of historic events. These are traditionally learnt by rote – off by heart. This can be an effective method, but it may not be as efficient as some of the alternatives explored in this section.

2. **Application or 'doing stuff with stuff we know'.** We apply knowledge when we solve equations or convert tables into something meaningful. This is like using the bricks of knowledge to create anything we're asked to build, such as houses, cathedrals or bridges.

Test yourself

1. Describe these two objects.

2. Compare these two objects as food.

We need to be able to demonstrate both
knowledge and the ability to evaluate information.

calculate interpret
describe locate
what paraphrase
who outline
why **knowledge comprehension** repeat
when define
where label find

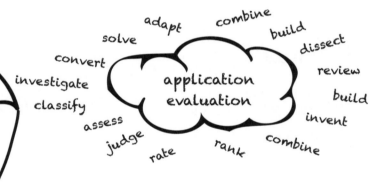

adapt combine
solve build
convert dissect
investigate review
classify **application evaluation** build
assess invent
judge rate rank combine

What is the scariest thing you've ever done?

Use the knowledge and comprehension words above to record
the experience.

Now record the same experience using the application and
evaluation words.

How are they different?

Remember: knowledge is like underwear – it's useful to have it, but you don't
necessarily need to show it off!

LEARNING AND REMEMBERING

Using SNOT in the classroom

When you get stuck, look for the answer in this order:

Self – don't ask for help immediately. If we're always given answers before we think about the problem fully, we never remember the answer long term or place knowledge into a wider context.

Neighbour – if you can't unstuck yourself then try asking your neighbour. Altogether now, 'Neighbours, everybody needs good neighbours. With a little understanding ...' and so on!

Other – move on to another person or resource, such as the Internet, a textbook, whiteboard or worksheet, before finally asking the teacher.

Teacher – this is the last resort not the first resort. Checking with self, other students or resources before the teacher should help you question and contextualise ideas and potential answers – which is great practice at application.

Extended acronyms

Mnemonics are most useful for remembering sequences of information of between five and nine items. For example:

* Colours of the spectrum: red, orange, yellow, green, blue, indigo, violet
  Richard Of York Gave Battle in Vain

* Planets from the sun: Mercury, Venus, Earth, Mars, Jupiter, Saturn, Uranus, Neptune, (Pluto)*
  My Very Easy Memory Jingle Seems Useful Naming Planets

Try your own for bones in the lower body: hip, femur, patella, tibia, fibula, tarsals, metatarsals and phalanges.

  H F P T F T M P

* In the olden days Tim and David were taught this mnemonic. More recently Pluto has been downgraded from a planet to a big bit of rock, hence the brackets. Most scientific ideas are changed over the centuries. In writing this book we're sharing the ideas, theory and research that has been most useful to the students with whom we've worked over the past fifteen years.

Visual associations

Here are some examples of visual associations.

✳ **The year penicillin was discovered:** Imagine a big Petri dish with disgusting green phlegmy bacteria growing all over the jelly except for a blank strip across the middle where the penicillin has killed the bacteria and in which is written 1928. The green phlegmy visual reminds us not only of the year of discovery but also the discoverer's name: Alexander Fleming.

✳ **The French word for a book (*un livre*):** Picture a book with a cover made of liver. Visualise the dark red slippery surface. Imagine picking it up and feeling it slip between your fingers. Repeat 'un livre' as you picture this.

✳ **Capital cities:** Qatar's capital city is Doha. We like to imagine Homer Simpson in a football strip (Qatar is hosting the 2022 FIFA World Cup) kicking a ball badly and muttering 'Doh!' It works for us!

Learning to spell the most commonly misspelt words will please not only your English teacher, but it will also impress examiners.

Which is correct – 'definitely' or 'definately'? Or 'accidentally' or 'accidently'?

For *definitely*, the *nit* in the middle can help – imagine you are checking for nits in your hair. Do the actions of combing your hair as you say 'I definitely have nits' a couple of times.

Try your own for 'accidentally'.

How many of these do you know? If you're not sure, check page 121 for the correct spellings.

Acceptible	Collum	Experiance	Libary	Relevent
Adquire	Foriegn	Innoculate	Medeival	Wierd

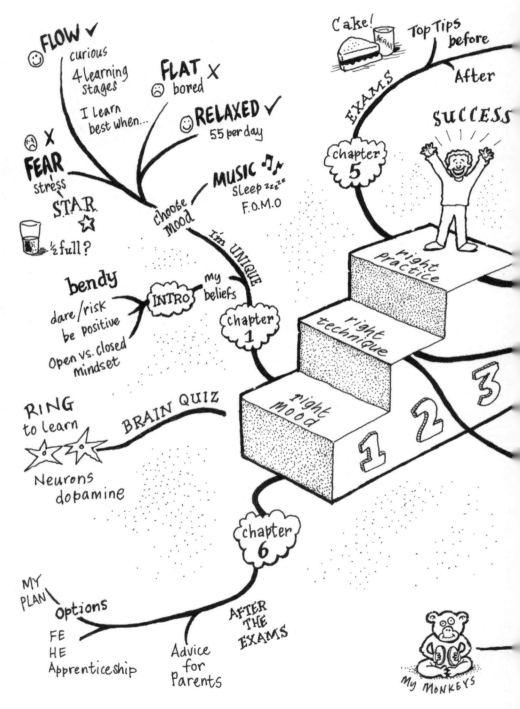

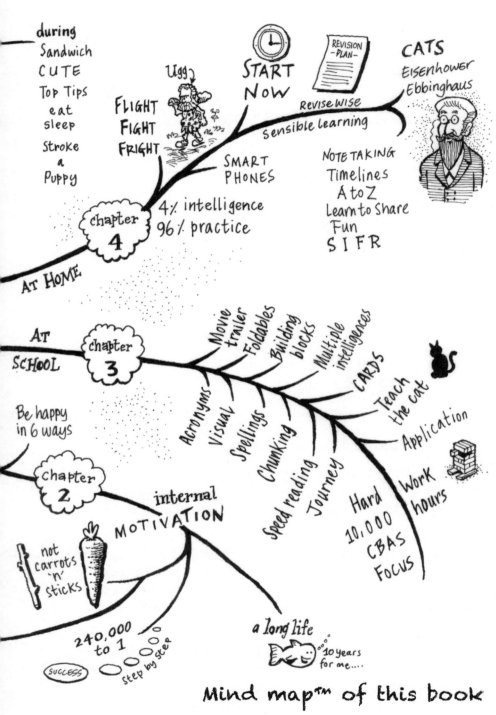

during
Sandwich
CUTE
Top Tips
eat
sleep
Stroke
a
Puppy

FLIGHT
FIGHT
FRIGHT

Ugg

START
Now

REVISION
-PLAN-

Revise Wise

Sensible learning

CATS
Eisenhower
Ebbinghaus

chapter
4

4% intelligence
96% practice

SMART
PHONES

NOTE TAKING
Timelines
A to Z
Learn to Share
Fun
S I F R

AT HOME

AT
SCHOOL

chapter
3

Movie
trailer

Foldables

Building
blocks

Multiple
intelligences

CARDS

Teach
the cat

Application

Be happy
in 6 ways

Acronyms

Visual

Spellings

Chunking

Speed reading

Journey

Hard
10,000
CBAS
Focus

Work
hours

chapter
2

internal
MOTIVATION

not
carrots
'n'
sticks

240,000
to 1

SUCCESS

step by step

a long life

10 years
for me....

Mind map™ of this book

81

Chunking

Mind maps™ are a visual form of chunking. We all learn things in different ways and at different levels. We tend to focus our attention in two directions though: up or down, big picture or detail. Our eyes are always looking through a microscope or a telescope. This is chunking.

When we can chunk a topic or subject, we demonstrate real understanding. For example, if someone asks you about the Second World War you might think, do they mean the causes, the main battles, the Blitz, rationing, the role of women working in factories, propaganda, the Enigma code or the role of the United States?

Chunking means you can link each piece of knowledge into a wider context. This displays deep knowledge and understanding. Test yourself by seeing if you can link pairs from the above list, such as rationing and propaganda (perhaps linked by wholesome recipe advertising campaigns).

Inside the Brain Box

The brain makes sense of the world by looking for patterns. It likes to make links between things. Meaning and insight are generated when new connections fire between our neurons.

Humans have always looked up at the clouds and seen dragons and faces in the random formations that drift along. Patterns seem to excite the brain and make the neurons dance. It is believed that spotting patterns and making predictions helped our ancestors to survive.

Tim looked up at the clouds the other day and saw a whale, a smiley face, Lord Voldemort, a chicken and the Falkland Islands in the cloud formations. What would our ancestors have made of that!

Inside the Brain Box

The eye sees far quicker than we read sentences. This is because, to some extent, we still read in the same slow way we were taught to read as young children. This is fine when we're 5, and just learning, but it wastes time when we're older. We can increase our reading speed, without losing meaning, by relying more on our eyes.

This experiment demonstrates how our eyes can read more than we think.

In the following sentence the order of the letters has been jumbled. If you read at normal speed you will still be able to recognise all of the words.

Eevn toghuh teh ltertes hvae bene mexid ot cusfnoe yuo, yuro alitiby ot regonisce wrod petartns adn manineg is peamnohenl.

Speed reading

If you are studying subjects that require lots of reading then this is a skill worth developing. Speed reading can save you serious amounts of time.

First, check your current reading speed. Read a random paragraph of around 15 lines at normal speed and time yourself. Work out your lines per minute, or words per minute if you're the competitive type.

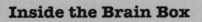

83

Easy speed reading

Enter the right mood, relaxed and focused ...

Spend a little time thinking about why you're going to read a chapter or web article. If you're holding a book, rather than looking at a screen, you can check out the chapter headings and subheadings. Which are most relevant? Start there. Never read a book chronologically if it's for research. (If it's a detective novel that you're reading for pleasure, then speed reading won't be appropriate!) What do you already know? Is there any specific information you're looking for?

Try to look at a whole page at once (start with paragraphs first to build up your speed), scanning each line of text really quickly. Look for important words and recognise them without trying to read whole sentences. Keep going and only stop to underline or note an important point. You should be able to treble your speed straight away.

Summarise the learning points at an appropriate time.

Journey method: themes of The Tempest

If you know where you left the memory, you'll know where to find it. It could even be around your own body ...

Try to visualise each of the objects listed opposite in as memorable way as possible – vivid colours, sounds, movements, textures, smells and tastes. The more memorable the description, the more likely you are to remember it – and where you left it.

MAGIC WAND

Magic (in ear)

A MASK

costume/theatre

WHIP Power/control

RECORDER Sounds/music (in mouth)

PILE OF DIRT earth (on shoulder)

GLASS OF SALT WATER water/sea

A BEE TRAIL betrayal

BEATING HEART forgiveness (between knees)

BALLOON air (down pants)

A BUTLER'S TRAY servant/master

85

Seven ways to make learning more interesting

How we learn as individuals differs from person to person. Identifying our own learning preferences can help us to study more effectively and efficiently.

As we've already seen, we remember things best when they combine pictures, words and feelings. Our most vivid and memorable moments are wired into our brain in the form of short movie trailer-style clips. In the jargon, that's visual (see), auditory (hear) and kinaesthetic (do).

Here are some of the best examples we've encountered that bring together all three.

Which ideas will work for you?

1. Movie trailer

Make a short clip for YouTube or your teacher/classmates using a smartphone or tablet. Use a series of key images or words written on sticky notes. Try filming in one take and do the voice-over as you move the sticky notes in and out of shot. The clip will also be a useful revision aid.

2. Building blocks

Buy a cheap, non-branded version of Jenga and write key concepts/words on each block.

Build the tower and play the game, testing yourself on each block you remove. Playing with friends will enhance the power of this game.

When the tower collapses, group blocks together in a sort of mind map or choose two random blocks and consider how they are linked.

3. Card shark

Take a deck of cards and write key
words, characters or phrases on
each card. Be imaginative. Here
are some suggestions:

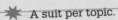

- ✳ A suit per topic.

- ✳ Picture cards could be key people.

- ✳ Quotes on aces.

- ✳ Each suit could run through the key scenes of a play or book plot.

- ✳ Each card could have a maths question on one side with the answer on the other.

- ✳ Numbers of cards could link directly to an idea or date.

Shuffle the cards and start revising.

Can you adapt any other board games for revision purposes?

4. Top Trumps

Some subjects lend themselves to the
Top Trumps approach, especially those
where you need to compare subjects or
themes (e.g. countries, books, people/
characters). Instead of giving scores for
each category, you could leave them
blank and argue the case for your card
against a friend. This is a great way to
share each other's knowledge.

5. Foldables

Hiding key information, concepts and formulae beneath flaps of paper is more exciting than it sounds! It also provides a welcome alternative to reading, rereading, note taking and a highlighter pen.

Here are four of our favourites:

1. Flaps one (using three A4 sheets)

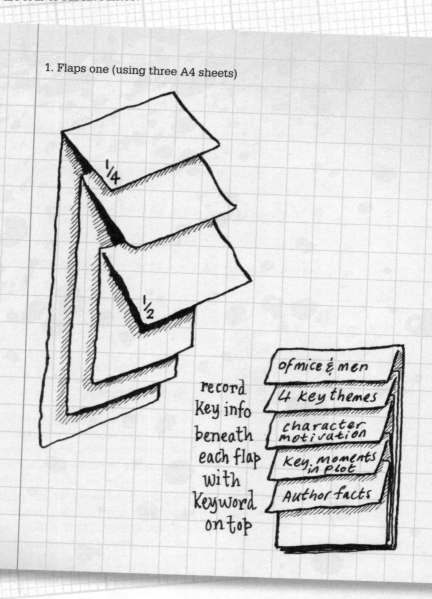

1/4

1/2

record
key info
beneath
each flap
with
keyword
on top

of mice & men

4 key themes

character
motivation

key moments
in plot

Author facts

① Break down topic into 4 key pieces of learning (**3** or **5** also works)

② 4 key themes
4 medical breakthroughs
4 main characters
(you get the idea)

③ write on 4 sheets of paper

④ write "trigger" word on reverse

⑤ Scrunch up each sheet into a ball

⑥ Throw into a target

clean bin!

⑦ Choose a paper ball at random and unscrunch

⑧ Look at trigger word and check how much you remember

ROMEO

⑨ Repeat process until your recall/memory is good

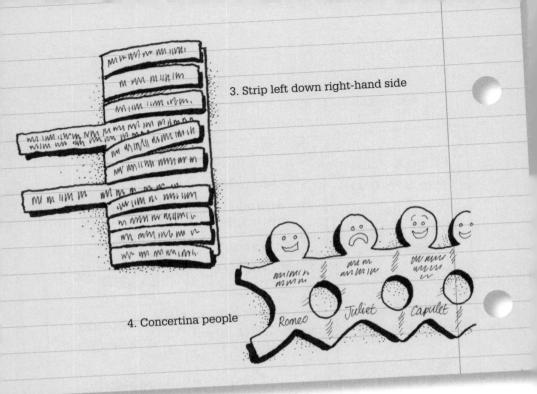

3. Strip left down right-hand side

4. Concertina people

Romeo   Juliet   Capulet

Multiple intelligences

The theory of multiple intelligences (which was developed by the psychologist Howard Gardner) suggests that there are eight different ways in which we express intelligence. Gardner calls these 'intelligences' and believes that they can be developed.

The eight intelligences are:

1. Words: read/write, be good at spelling, think in words/ poetry/lyrics.

2. Numbers: puzzles, abstract ideas, theory, quizzes, tests, asking 'why?'

3. Pictures: think in images, pictures, maps, diagrams, colours.

4. Music: sing, hum, remember melodies, like to hear music as you work.

5. Body: remember via feelings, sport, drama, dance, coordination, learn through movement, role play, games.

6. People: socialise, mediate, good listener, read moods well.

7. Nature: affinity with the natural world, like being outdoors, classifying and categorising plants/animals.

8. Self: know self, independent, value own strengths, aims, goals and opinions.

Exploring a topic using the eight multiple intelligences can be a satisfying way to digest the key learning points.

Take your topic and summarise it in eight different ways:

1. Words: research/write a poem/find a speech/choose 6–15 words to summarise the topic.

2. Numbers: identify the five most important points.

3. Pictures: find five key icons/photographs/pictures to arrange as an exhibition.

4. Music: choose three songs that make you think about the topic.

5. Body: create/perform sporting analogies.

6. People: create a Facebook profile for three major people involved in the topic.

7. Nature: explore an environmental impact of the topic.

8. Self: how would you have behaved differently to the three key people you have selected?

6. Teaching the cat

There's a saying that we never really *understand* something until we have to *teach* it.

Break down the stuff you need to learn into chunks and teach it to someone else. If you have friends studying the same subjects you can teach each other. If you struggle with fractions but understand algebra, and your friend is the other way round, you could help one another by first teaching each other what you know and then swapping, just to make sure you understand.

If you have no friends, you can teach an imaginary friend, the cat or a favourite soft toy. It is much better to teach real people, though, as they're good at asking for clarification on the bits you know least well – which helps you learn it. They'll also ask you to rephrase stuff, which will help you to learn at a deeper level.

This table shows why the teaching the cat method works.

Can you match the percentage of content we remember with the way we experience it?*

Lecture	50%
Reading	90%
A good PowerPoint	5%
Discuss in a group	20%
Practice by doing	10%
Teaching others	75%

* Answers: lecture – 5%, reading – 10%, a good PowerPoint – 20%, discuss in a group – 50%, practice by doing – 75%, teaching others – 90%.

7. Application

To check you really understand something, you can challenge yourself, or a friend, to find random connections. For example, when my daughter was studying John Steinbeck's *Of Mice and Men*, I asked her, 'What does it have in common with the programme *Call the Midwife*?' She thought for a while and suggested that the levels of vocabulary used by the characters reflected their level of education and ability to make rational decisions. This application helped to cement her learning.

So, how is *Of Mice and Men* like:

✳ School?

✳ A fridge?

✳ Chicken curry?

Thinking about things differently or creatively is more memorable!

The 80/20 rule for revision

The Pareto principle states that 80% of our rewards come from 20% of our work or effort.

It applies across many disciplines. If we spend a little time thinking about how to best use our time for maximum effort, we will reap the rewards.

We are often tempted to look over the stuff we already know and like, rather than diving into the messy areas of our knowledge and interest.

Revisiting the material you already know pretty well for two hours may gain you an extra 2% in an exam. Looking over the stuff you struggle with for two hours could bring you an extra 10%. Apply this principle in subjects or topics within subjects.

What area of revision should you focus on for maximum benefit?

Write down your thoughts.

If the suggestions sound just as wise tomorrow, then off you go!

HARD WORK

We seem to live in a culture where we expect to get everything we want straight away.

No one is prepared to wait for things. We don't save up – we just use credit.

Musicians find instant fame on reality TV without learning their trade on the road or suffering failure but bouncing back stronger and wiser.

In school, if we don't 'get it' immediately, there is a tendency to say 'It's too hard' or 'I can't do it' and give up.

But this isn't the path to success or even the path to being good at something.

If it's not now, it's *never*.

If you look at someone who is a success – *really* a success, not *X Factor* successful – you will find that they have worked, slogged, practised, honed and trained for a long time. They will have experienced really tough times, but kept going. They will have failed, but picked themselves up and started again.

One Direction are one of the few exceptions (they came third on *The X Factor* in 2010); most talent show winners quickly sink into obscurity. In the past, bands served a long 'apprenticeship' by playing small venues, often for many years, and honing their talent. When they finally break through, their years of hard graft help sustain a long career based on skill and practice. The Beatles, arguably the biggest boy band of all time, found success by playing long shows in the beer halls of Hamburg. They played more than 250 gigs between 1960 and 1962, some of which were eight-hour sets. They became successful because they worked at it.

The kids who get 10 As aren't always the brightest, but they usually work the hardest.

If you think you can start your revision two weeks before the exams, having slacked off for the previous two years, and still get top grades, then you're in for a shock.

You can't!

Inside the Brain Box

What makes someone an expert?

One man set out to answer this question. The Swedish psychologist, Professor K. Anders Ericsson, wanted to discover what it takes to become truly successful in any given field. He conducted his research on violinists at the Berlin Music Academy and found that it takes roughly 10,000 hours to master a skill.

There are no naturals; it is purely about the work we put in.

Experience is everything. The more you do, the better you get. Start young. Work hard. Be focused. Avoid distractions. It won't necessarily mean you're happy, but if you want something badly enough, you need to work for it.

'Mozart was not born an expert,' Professor Ericsson wrote, 'he became one!' 10,000 hours is about four hours a day, five days a week, for ten years! Blimey!

No one has yet found a case in which true world class expertise was accomplished in less time [10,000 hours]. It seems it takes the brain this long to assimilate all it needs to know to achieve true mastery.
Professor Daniel Levitin, psychologist and neurologist

The challenging life of Abraham Lincoln

✴ Age 22 he failed in business.

✴ Age 23 he was defeated in local elections.

✴ Age 24 he failed in business again.

✴ Age 25 he was elected to the state legislature.

✴ Age 29 he was defeated as Speaker.

✴ Age 31 he was defeated for unpledged elector.

✴ Age 34 he was defeated for Congress.

✴ Age 37 he was elected to Congress.

✴ Age 39 he was defeated for Congress.

✴ Age 46 he was defeated for the Senate.

✴ Age 47 he was defeated for Vice-President.

✴ Age 49 he was defeated for the Senate.

✴ Age 51 he was elected President of the United States of America!

What if he'd given up?

10,000 is the magic number!

Grandmaster

Garry Kasparov, the world's youngest ever chess Grandmaster, was ranked No. 1 in the world for 255 months. Many consider him the greatest chess player of all time. He started playing chess from a very young age and enrolled in chess classes from the age of 7. By the age of 15, he was already ranked No. 2 in the world!

How did he get that good? He put in the hours.

HAVE YOU GOT CBAS?

There is a very serious condition that affects a lot of people. It is endemic and there is no known cure.

The condition is CBAS – Can't Be Arsed Syndrome.

It's very serious. You may have it. Let's do a quick diagnosis.

When your mum asks you to help with the washing up, do you think, 'Oh, I can't be bothered with that'? If so, you may have CBAS.

What about tidying your bedroom? Do you often feel like doing it? No? Do you *never* want to do it because it's way too much effort? Yes? Then it's probably because you have CBAS.

You have loads of homework to do, but all you can manage is to lie on the sofa watching telly. You have CBAS!

CBAS happens in class too.

The teacher asks a question and no one puts up their hand (because they all have CBAS too!). So the teacher picks on someone. They say in a really bored voice, 'I dunno.'

The teacher then picks on someone else. 'I don't know.'

Someone else gets asked, but it's the same thing: 'Dunno,' 'Dunno,' 'Dunno.'

This is CBAS in action.

Sometimes people genuinely don't know the answer. That's OK. If we knew everything, we wouldn't need to be in school!

So, you don't *know*, but what do you *think*?

All answers are good, even if they're not necessarily correct.

The only wrong answer is 'I don't know' because it shows: (a) you aren't thinking and (b) you have CBAS.

Because of CBAS, the average time between a teacher asking a question and giving the answer is ... anyone?

Between one and three seconds.

If your teachers are telling you the answers, it's like spoon-feeding.

Try thinking about this question right now: where might day and night be found together?

Can you come up with at least 20 ideas?

If you can, you've probably tackled the problem from different angles – it's what we call divergent thinking. Employers and universities like this.

They *don't* want people with CBAS.

They *don't* want people who expect to be told the answers.

They *don't* want people who give up as soon as it gets tough.

They *do* want people who are creative in their thinking.

They *do* want people who aren't afraid to get it wrong.

They *do* want people who can THINK for themselves.

Is that you?

(Don't say, 'I don't know.')

Remember: only babies need to be spoon-fed.

ARE YOU WORKING WELL IN CLASS?

In a moment we're going to ask you to think of a number.

It will be a two-digit number and the digits will not be the same.

Nearly ready?

OK, the number is odd and is between 19 and 60.

Now quickly think of the number.

Write it down here and we'll see if we can predict it shortly.

When we're nervous, we tend to be quite predictable. If you ask someone to quickly name a colour, most say red. If asked to name a vegetable, most will say carrot.

OK, was the number 37?

Try it for yourself. You will find that a majority of people say 37. This is because we naturally go into auto-pilot thinking, and 3 and 7 are the first odd numbers we're likely to retrieve when we're put on the spot.

How are you working in class?

If you're in auto-pilot mode, you'll be nowhere near your peak.

Make sure you're on your toes and at your best to avoid your work being red carrots!

Are you ever going to achieve your potential if you're giving it only half your effort, or less?

Intelligence is a factor, but mostly it comes down to how well you work. Those who work hard or smart tend to do better.

Do some work!

FOCUS

Just how good is your focus?

What can you hear right now? There is probably some really obvious noise.
But if you focus your hearing and *really* listen, you may well be surprised at what else you can hear.

Sometimes we tune in, sometimes we tune out …

In class, it's really easy to tune in to the wrong things – what our friend is saying, what's on your phone under the desk, what's happening outside the window.

It's easy to tune out the important stuff – like what the teacher is saying or doing.

Focus is a choice.

Focus is about not talking about things that have nothing to do with the learning whilst ignoring the important stuff.

Focus is about active listening – making notes, asking questions, tuning in.

Focus is about making eye contact with the person who is speaking.

Focus is about staying on task and ignoring distractions.

You know what really makes the difference between a student who gets an A and a student who gets a C or a D?

Is it intelligence? No.

It's focus.

If you want to do well, learn how to focus.

Work smart, not hard.

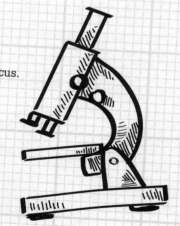

Mini brain upgrade: new day resolution

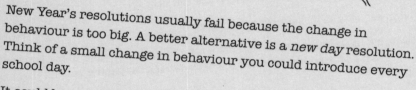

Around 40% of people make New Year's resolutions. Only 12% manage to keep them!

How is your willpower?

New Year's resolutions usually fail because the change in behaviour is too big. A better alternative is a *new day* resolution. Think of a small change in behaviour you could introduce every school day.

It could be to read through notes at home made that day at school in one key subject and highlight one key point. Continue the new behaviour for a term, then keep it or start another. Set it as a reminder on your phone to ensure you don't lapse.

SUMMARY

Tick the box if you agree:

- ☐ We need to 'learn to learn' in order to make the best of school.
- ☐ Sometimes we need to knuckle down and do some hard work.
- ☐ To be great at something needs effort.
- ☐ It's no good being lazy.
- ☐ If you are spoon-fed, you aren't developing your own abilities.
- ☐ It's good to tune out distractions and focus on important things.
- ☐ The right attitude leads to the right results.

CHAPTER 4

AT HOME
DEALING WITH REVISION

LET'S GET PERSONAL ...

Have you got a signature? If so, how do you sign your name? You'll do it thousands of times during your lifetime, so have a good one.

Sign your name here:

So, how was that? Easy? Comfortable? Natural?

Now put your pen in the other hand – the one you don't normally write with – and sign your name again.

How was that? Hard? Uncomfortable? Awkward?

Sometimes we try to work in ways that don't suit us. We might be asked to work using approaches that make us feel uncomfortable or awkward.

It's the same with revision. Some methods will be perfect for us. Others will just feel weird. Use the techniques that feel right. Don't do the ones that feel odd. Simple.

RIGHT PRACTICE

Intelligence is overrated.

So what is *real intelligence*?

Top surgeons don't have higher IQ's, better exam scores or superior manual dexterity than average surgeons.

Grandmaster chess players don't have higher IQs than average chess players.

In general, intelligence accounts for 4% of variability in performance.

96% is down to practice.

Quick intelligence test

Does the world seem to be getting bigger and funnier all the time?

If it does, then your *intelligence* is steadily increasing.

Or, does the world seem to be getting smaller and nastier all the time?

If so, your *stupidity* is steadily increasing.

(*Source*: Simon Moon (aka Robert Anton Wilson), 'Stupidynamics')

Focus on the main thing

Have you noticed how we'll happily tidy our room, wash up, check Facebook or walk the dog rather than start work?

How much time do you waste on distractions?

Conduct a mini research project on yourself. In a one-hour work slot, record how much time you *actually* spend on task.

> The main thing is to keep the main thing the main thing.
> Stephen Covey

UGG THE CAVEMAN

Ugg the Caveman had been hunting and gathering all day. But he had caught NOTHING. Worst caveman EVER.

He was stressed...

.... and hungry.

RUMBLE

All he could find to eat, which wouldn't run away, were the berries on a bush. Only pick the blue berries, Ugg! The red ones are poisonous!

But Ugg was not alone........

Suddenly a mighty Sabre-toothed tiger leapt from the bushes!

ROAR!

What will Ugg the caveman do?

Well, potentially Ugg will respond in a number of ways, all of which will be instinctive.

His senses will warn him of the immediate danger and adrenalin will be released into his bloodstream. The adrenalin will rush to his limbs making him buff and far stronger and quicker than normal!

This equips him for two things:

FIGHT – his instinct will tell him to fight for his life.

AIEEEE!!

Or **FLIGHT** – he may just run away!

Ugg may also **freeze**, unable to think what to do.

This may seem daft, but it might actually help him live. If he was fully capable of thinking clearly, he may decide to throw the poisonous red berries at

the sabre-toothed tiger. This won't work because the tiger will now not only be hungry but a little bit annoyed as well.

Ugg will get eaten.

If Ugg is frozen, there is a chance that the sabre-toothed tiger may not see him and wander off to eat someone, or something else, instead.

So, stress can make us do these three things: fight, flight or freeze. What's that got to do with revision?

Exams are your sabre-toothed tiger! Exams make us stressed! Because we are stressed, we will show one, two or all three of the stress responses.

Fight!

Being stressed can make us snappy and stroppy!

Do you get aggressive when you're stressed? Many people do. Be aware of this as your exams get closer. Talk about your stress. Get some exercise. Let off steam. You'll feel better. Don't just shout at people. Or punch things. Or people.

Flight!

Wow! You've got loads of stuff to learn for your exams. That's pretty stressful. There seems to be a huge pile to learn.

Are you tackling it or avoiding it? Are you head on or head in the sand?

The more you run away and procrastinate, the more stressed you'll become. The hardest part of revision is starting.

Your stress will make you avoid it. Once you begin, though, the stress will start to reduce.

Begin today, if you haven't already. Start NOW! Do SOMETHING!

Freeze!

Ever panicked in an exam then come out and known what you should have written? That's the freeze.

Ever tried to ask someone out and been massively tongue tied? That's the freeze.

Ever had a job interview and not known what to say? That's the freeze!

The more revision you do, the more confident you'll feel and the less nervous you'll become. The less nervous you are, the less likely you are to freeze.

So, when it comes to revision, are you guilty of fight, flight or freeze?

Are you a fighter?

I can fix my aggression in three ways:

1.

2.

3.

Are you a runner?

Three things to help me start revision:

1.

2.

3.

Are you freezing?

No need for panic! Here are three things I've remembered from revision that I've done in the last week:

1.

2.

3.

GET READY TO WORK ...

So, the hardest thing about revising is starting. We often put off revision because it scares us or we don't know how to do it.

Let's get this sorted right now. You need to revise. You need to start.

On your busiest day, how much, realistically, could you do?

Don't say 'nothing'. You could fit in some revision.

But how much?

An hour? Maybe that's too much.

Half an hour? No – still unrealistic.

Fifteen minutes?

Come on! That's next to nothing.

Ten minutes? Well, that's still better than nothing.

So how much could you do?

Write it here:

....

This is your minimum revision commitment, six days a week. It doesn't matter what else happens, you have to commit to doing this much each day.*

Let's say it's 15 minutes (because we could all do that).

That's one-and-a-half-hours of revision each week that you weren't doing before. That will help (equally, if you wrote 30 minutes that will be three hours a week, if an hour then it will be six hours of revision and so on).

Brilliant!

So, you do your 15 minutes. Then what?

Well, if you have no more time, then you're done.

Go and do what you need to do, without guilt. You've achieved your goal. Well done.

But ...

You might find 15 minutes was easy. You learnt some stuff and you think you could do a bit more, and you have some time. Great! Do it! Do as much as you feel you can – it will all help. The more you invest, the greater your knowledge.

Just make sure you do your minimum each day. This way you establish the habit. You'll be making progress.

At the end of each week, examine your goal – could you raise the minimum? Should you do more each day? Do you need to?

Always be honest with yourself.

Stick to your goal. Do the minimum – and more if you can. But always do the amount you wrote above.

Don't argue. Just enjoy it.

Seriously, though, some of you are working really hard. That's great, but we all need some time out. You'll need it.

You'll unwind.

You'll recharge.

You'll process what you've already learnt.

You'll have fun.

So take a day off each week. A day for you.

Enjoy!

* Now some good news: only do this six days a week – have at least one day off.

Inside the Brain Box

Experts seem to think, as a rough rule, that our concentration span is our age plus or minus one or two minutes.

Therefore it's good to revise in chunks of around 15 minutes.

In one hour, you would revise for 15 minutes and then have a 5-minute break.

Then revise for another 15 minutes, followed by a 5-minute break.

And then finish with another 15 minutes.

In every hour, you should aim to work for 45 minutes. At the end of an hour, have a slightly longer break, say 10–20 minutes, and then start again.

But remember: we're all different, so work out what is best for you. Then try to stick to it.

The more you work, the longer your concentration span will become. Try to extend the time you revise – so start with 10 minutes, then extend to 15, then 20.

Never try to revise for more than 45 minutes in one go. Take regular breaks – go and do something you enjoy.

> I always revise the stuff I know – it makes me feel better.
> Year 11 student

Revising what you already know isn't the way to do it. But many of us fall into this error.

We tend to revise the subjects we like!

Why? It's easier. It makes us feel better. It's more enjoyable.

The trouble is, we probably know that stuff already.

So, we need a structure – something to help us revise. A plan! We need a way to make sure we're revising *everything*.

Here are two great methods for creating a revision planner to help you keep on task and cover everything.

The traditional revision planner

	MONDAY	TUESDAY	WEDNESDAY	THURSDAY	FRIDAY	SATURDAY AM	SATURDAY PM
HISTORY	CAUSES OF WWI	TREATY OF VERSAILLES	LEAGUE OF NATIONS	ROAD TO WWII	WEIMAR GERMANY	RUSSIA 1905-1941	COLD WAR
SCIENCE	METALS	HEATING AND COOLING	ELECTRICITY	OIL AND FUELS	FOOD CHAINS	NERVES AND HORMONES	BODY AND HEALTH
GEOGRAPHY	WEATHER	WATERS AND RIVERS	COASTS	MIGRATION	TOURISM	SUSTAINABILITY	GLOBALISATION
RE	WAR & PEACE	GOD	SANCTITY OF LIFE	CHRISTIANITY	JUDAISM	SIKHISM	ISLAM
PE	NUTRITION	HUMAN BODY	PARTICIPATION	HEALTH AND FITNESS	DRUGS IN SPORT	PERFORMANCE ANALYSIS	SAFETY AND RISK
ENGLISH LITERATURE	CRUCIBLE	MICE AND MEN	ROMEO AND JULIET	POETRY	SHORT STORIES	ANIMAL FARM	
MATHS/ ENGLISH PAST PAPER PRACTICE	YES - ENGLISH		YES - MATHS			YES - ENGLISH	YES - MATHS

REPEAT EVERY WEEK UNTIL THE EXAMS

This is easy. It works like a diary.

You work out how long you have until your exams.

You work out what you need to learn.

You decide what you want to revise on each day.

You stick to it.

You do well.

The drawbacks are:

1. You might spend three weeks creating the revision planner. With gel pens. When you've finished it, you may realise that there's no time left to revise.

2. What if you don't stick to it?

If you can stick to it, this is a good method. If you can't stick to it, because your life is a bit random or chaotic, then the following approach may suit you better.

The alternative revision planner

First, make a long list of everything you need to revise – all the topics within each subject.

Then create a grid like the one above (you'll need enough boxes for every topic). This won't include specific dates – just lots of blank boxes.

Next, write a topic in each box.

In your first 15 minute revision session, choose a box, revise the topic, then tick the box and date it. Then choose another box, revise the topic, tick it and date it.

The next day revisit these boxes. Tick and date them again. Revise stuff in other boxes using the same process and tick/date them.

Once you've revised a topic, you'll be able to see when you need to look at it again, at the following intervals:

- ✷ 24 hours
- ✷ Three days
- ✷ One week
- ✷ Three weeks
- ✷ Once a month until near your exam

Then look at each topic regularly before the actual exam, and cram at the last moment. If you miss a day, just pick up where you left off.

At any point you can see:

(a) What you've already revised.

(b) When you need to look at a topic again.

(c) What you have yet to revise.

(d) Whether you are working hard enough.

(e) Whether you need to up your revision.

Choose one of these two great methods and stick to them.

Remember: don't just revise the stuff you already know.

HOW DO I REVISE?

Or more importantly, how do *you* like to learn?

As we've seen, we're all different and like to learn/revise in different ways.

Which of these statements most applies to you?

(a) I like to see things – graphs, lists, pictures, diagrams. I like my information presented in a visual way.

(b) I like things to be explained to me. I like to either hear it or read it. I like my information presented with words.

If you are an (a) person, then you learn best when there are a lot of images. For you, it's about *mind maps*, *doodles* and little *drawings*, *videos* and *pictures*. You will probably be drawn to the images in this book, but won't focus so much on the chunks of text.

If you are a (b) person, you learn best from *reading* and *listening*. Give you the book and you'll work it out. You like an *explanation*. When you're given one, you'll get it. You may well be reading the longer passages here in *The Brain Box*.

If you're an (a), work on your *listening skills*. Try *note taking* and *explaining* things to other people. Focus on what is being said – ask *questions* and write down *keywords*.

If you're a (b), try summarising information in visual form. You'll be able to access it quicker next time. Try *doodling* or *mind-mapping* as you go along. Use *colour*.

What about these two statements? Which of these most applies to you?

(a) I like to learn by doing. I enjoy trial and error. I am practical. I enjoy working with others to solve a problem.

(b) I prefer to reflect and think about things. I like to see the evidence and draw my own conclusions. I prefer to work things out on my own.

If you're an (a), you will find it difficult to revise in isolation. You will prefer hands-on revision strategies and enjoy working in *study groups*. When revising alone, you'll often find yourself getting distracted and going off to do other things.

If you're a (b), on the other hand, you will prefer to *revise alone* and will get more done on your own. You don't mind being *isolated* and will actually get distracted and annoyed by others around you when you're trying to work.

Sense-ible learning!

You've got five different senses. Use them when you're revising.

1. **Sight** – pictures, doodles, videos, images, words, diagrams, lines, colours, drawings

2. **Hearing** – explanations, listening to others, podcasts, music, making up songs or rhymes to help you remember

3. **Smell** – scented candles when you are working, scented pens, coffee brewing in the next room for when you are ready for a break, scented paper

4. **Taste** – rewarding yourself with snacks or sweets when you're working, eating fruit for brain food!

5. **Touch** – stress balls, favourite cushion, moving Q&A cards around, thinking walks, playing ball games whilst others test you

Making notes

When you're making notes, make sure you include a range of visual stimuli:

✳ Words
✳ Pictures
✳ Underlining
✳ Pictures
✳ Mind maps (with pictures)
✳ Pictures
✳ Doodles
✳ Flash cards
✳ Pictures
✳ Highlighting
✳ Colours
✳ Pictures
✳ Sticky notes
✳ Pictures
✳ Pictures
✳ Pictures

Time lines

Here's a good method ...

ROMANS INVADE BRITAIN – LOTS OF ROADS BUILT AND A BIG WALL BETWEEN ENGLAND AND SCOTLAND

ROMANS LEAVE – BRITAIN ENTERS THE DARK AGES. ROADS GET WORSE, FEWER MOSAICS.

MEDIEVAL AGE. A LOT OF VERY POOR PERSONAL HYGIENE ISSUES AFFECT BRITAIN.

HENRY VIII BECOMES KING, WIVES BECOME NERVOUS, THEN HIS CHILDREN TAKE OVER: EDWARD, MARY AND ELIZABETH I – ENGLAND'S GOLDEN AGE.

AFTER QUEEN ANNE, LOTS OF CHAPS CALLED GEORGE SIT ON THE THROWN. BUILDINGS START TO LOOK GOOD.

CHARLES II COMES BACK FROM FRANCE. ENGLAND DANCES AGAIN.

CIVIL WAR. CHARLES I BEHEADED, OLIVER CROMWELL BANS DANCING.

BIG SCRAP WITH NAPOLEON. ENGLAND FALLS OUT WITH FRANCE. AGAIN.

VICTORIA SITS ON THE THRONE FOR A VERY LONG TIME. EMPIRE IS BUILT. INDUSTRIAL AGE KICKS IN BIG TIME.

WORLD WAR I. VERY BAD TIME FOR EVERYONE.

WWII. HAVE WE NOT LEARNT?

POST WAR: RATIONING ELIZABETH II, ENGLAND WINS WORLD CUP AND CELEBRATES FOR 50 YEARS.

TODAY!

Draw out some time lines on a long sheet on paper. These will be effective for plotting the following:

✳ The way a river flows or the development of a river valley

✳ The narrative of a novel

✳ Historical events

✳ A scientific process

✳ A character's development, either in history or literature

Check out seven ways to make learning fun on page 86.

Think you've learnt a topic? It's good to test yourself in creative ways. It helps things stick.

So, below there is an A to Z list. Once you've learnt a topic, try to write down something about it next to each letter.

Some letters will be easy, others hard. But you'll remember far more by trying to think of something for each letter. Creative stuff stays with you.

Give it a go …

A ....

B ....

C ....

D ....

E ....

F ....

G ....

H ....

I ....

J ....

K ....

L ....

M ....

N ....

O ....

P ....

Q ....

R ....

S ....

T ....

U ....

V ....

W ....

X ....

Y ....

Z ....

Embrace your inner artist

Baz was a good artist. He also liked animals. So Baz drew a big picture of a zoo.

He then wrote revision notes on the picture.

The big ideas, those he didn't want to forget, he wrote around the elephants (because elephants never forget!).

The brightest ideas, he jotted down next to the flamingos.

Silly but important stuff went by the monkeys.

Phrases to remember were written by the parrots.

Key points to look out for went in the meerkat enclosure.

And so on.

Baz would add to the picture every day at school, take it home and stick it on his wall. He'd test himself to see if he could remember what he'd written where.

After his exam, Baz said: 'I could remember exactly what I'd written next to which animal.'

There are four reasons why this worked:

1. **Structure** – all learning needs structure. That's why teachers have lesson plans and revisers need a revision planner. The structure here was the zoo.

2. **Imagery** – because pictures are memorable. If we can link images with facts, we learn better.

3. **Fun** – because if we enjoy something, we learn it.

4. **Review** – from the Latin, and literally meaning 'to look through'. The more we look through things and review them, the more we remember.

This is old wisdom from the ancient Greeks, refined by St Thomas Aquinas, which has been passed down through the generations.

Get some big poster-style revision sheets on the wall. Add to them as you go along. Use lots of colour and pictures.

Tim says:

One student I met told me that she had a massive poster of her favourite pop star on the wall of her room. When she was making revision notes, she wrote them directly on the poster. She seemed to remember what she'd written and where!

Another lad, in the same class, heard this and announced that from now on he'd be making revision notes on his *Hollyoaks Babes* calendar!

If it works, it works.

You could do the same thing: revise today with your favourite hottie.

Tear and share!

It's good to work together.

A problem shared is a problem halved.

So, divide up the work and put your heads together. You learn one bit. Your mate can learn another bit.

Then come back together and teach each other. You'll learn well this way because:

(a) You have to teach it.

(b) It is easier to learn from our friends than on our own.

However, it is also important to spend time alone. Some things will go in far easier if you find a quiet place, get your head down and go for it in your own space.

To revise effectively, mix up working alone and working with others.

See it! Hear it! Say it! Do it!

WRITING AN ESSAY IN EIGHT STEPS: THE SHERLOCK HOLMES APPROACH

As you revise, you'll practise writing essays and preparing essay answers. If you're still studying, you may be required to write essays for assessment. Here is a practical way to approach planning these answers.

Start – study the question. Start by making sure you really do understand the question. Are there any words in the question that are confusing or ambiguous? Only when you are comfortable with the question should you start researching your topic.

Harness – hassle and harry for the evidence. Imagine you are Sherlock Holmes with every foggy corner of London on his radar. Be determined to collect every relevant fact or piece of information. Use the Internet, academic databases, the library and DVDs. As you gather evidence, remain in a curious and fascinated mood.

Evaluate – imagine you've sent all the information you've gathered to the lab to be forensically analysed. Sherlock did this in his own study, as he worked in the days before crime scene investigation teams were invented. Organise the information logically. Is there an obvious structure, such as for and against, or a timeline approach? The essay question often suggests a structure. Look for gaps in your knowledge and then go back and plug these.

Reflect – every detective ponders the evidence. They step back and allow the pieces to fall into place. Ask yourself questions about the subject from different viewpoints. What would characters in a play say about your thoughts so far? What would a TV interviewer ask you about your essay? Identify your best ideas. What are your main points? Take a break from thinking about the essay – new thoughts may bubble up to the surface if you give yourself a bit of space.

List – summarise your thoughts on paper. Use bullet points to outline the key points of your essay. If you do this on cards or sticky notes, you'll be able to move the order around if necessary. Make sure it flows. Leave stuff out that doesn't fit. It can be tempting to try and squeeze everything you've read into the essay, but if it's not relevant it's better to leave it out.

Orate – a great way to keep an essay fresh is to imagine you are speaking your thoughts to a group of trusted friends, people unfamiliar with the content but interested enough to listen to your thoughts. Sherlock Holmes used Dr Watson for this role.

Chunk – each chunk of information should be presented in individual paragraphs. These are single ideas that support your argument. Include each relevant point with at least one piece of evidence to back it up. If the evidence is controversial and disputed then say so. If you can add statistics and quotes, they will support your case.

Keep – retain your concentration all the way to the conclusion. Summarise your thoughts. If appropriate, state which side of the argument you favour. Finish with a big thought, quotation or interesting statistic.

Read through, correcting the grammar, making sentences flow and giving it balance. Proofread to eradicate silly mistakes. Check spelling mistakes by reading sentences backwards as we see individual words better that way. Reference your essay fully (unless in an exam) using the system agreed with your teacher.

Elementary, my dear Watson!

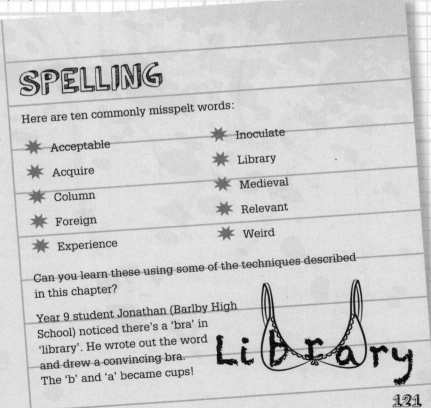

SPELLING

Here are ten commonly misspelt words:

* Acceptable
* Acquire
* Column
* Foreign
* Experience
* Inoculate
* Library
* Medieval
* Relevant
* Weird

Can you learn these using some of the techniques described in this chapter?

Year 9 student Jonathan (Barlby High School) noticed there's a 'bra' in 'library'. He wrote out the word and drew a convincing bra. The 'b' and 'a' became cups!

HOW TO REVISE MIGRATION ON YOUR HAND!

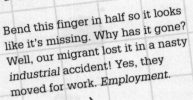

Bend this finger in half so it looks like it's missing. Why has it gone? Well, our migrant lost it in a nasty industrial accident! Yes, they moved for work. *Employment.*

What do we wear here? Wedding ring! What does that symbolise? Marriage! What is that about? Love? No! Misery and hardship (not in ours, obviously!). War, famine, pestilence, disease, floods, earthquakes … all the *disasters* that force people to move.

Point to your mouth and say 'Deeerrrrrrr', sounding as stupid as possible. *Education!* People become migrants to get educated.

Join the tip of your little finger to the tip of your thumb to make an 'O' shape. This is the O of *opportunity*. Migrants move for opportunities they would not have at home – health care, entertainment, being with family members.

Thumbs up and say, in a broad West Country accent, 'I lives in a brick house, I do!' *Better standard of living.* No longer in a mud hut in the country, our migrant lives in a better house, with a better life.

What other actions can you do with a hand?

You can do a 'push' action or a 'pull' action.

There are factors that push people to migrate (e.g. disasters) and factors that pull them (e.g. work opportunities, better standard of living).

What else could you learn like this?

Index cards

Small cards, the size of a postcard, are great for this technique.

You can use them in two ways:

1. Summarise key points – they're handy to carry around, and once you've learnt a topic, you can condense what you've learnt onto the back of a postcard.

2. Write questions on one side and answers on the other – then use them for others to test you.

You can also lend your cards to a friend and they can lend you their cards. Test each other and share the work.

STUDY BUDDY

Two heads are better than one!

Find someone who is studying what you're studying and agree to be each other's study buddy.

Essentially, they are your sponsor.

They have permission to have a go at you if you aren't working.

They can test you.

You can revise together.

You can share resources.

Don't go it alone. Get a study buddy! Everyone needs a good friend to help them out.

What will your study buddy be to you?

QUESTIONS, QUESTIONS, QUESTIONS (AND ANSWERS TOO, HOPEFULLY!)

The exams will be all about questions.

Get hold of some past papers and practise writing answers.

Why not get ten questions you can't answer yet and write down the questions in big letters on a sheet of paper? Maybe stick this on your wall.

As you're revising, keep looking back at the questions, working out if and how you can answer them.

TEN SMART WAYS TO USE YOUR SMARTPHONE

1. **Revision Buddies** – this is one of many revision apps that can be downloaded. Multiple-choice quizzes for different syllabuses and past paper questions are also available. Revision on the go! You could also try the Collins Revision App, Learner's Cloud, GCSE Pod or Ultimate Revision App. New revision apps become available all the time so, search, download and revise on the go.

2. **Audiobooks** – download the audiobook. Listen on the bus, the car or the train.

3. **Evernote** – this app enables you to keep your notes in one place, add web links, photos, etc., and use them across different platforms (e.g. phone, tablet, laptop).

4. **Simple Mind** – a mind-mapping tool that turns your phone into a device for brainstorming, ideas collection and thought structuring. Mind mapping in the palm of your hand!

5. **MP3s** – make audio notes and then splice them into playlists of your favourite tunes. A few tracks, a bit of audio, a few more tracks, a bit of audio and so on.

6. **Tweet your mates** – 140 characters is a great way of condensing what you've learnt. Set up a group hashtag and share gems of knowledge.

7. **iTunes** – revise for five songs, then take a break for two songs. Repeat.

8. **Video camera** – film your teacher explaining something really important. Watch it back. Again. Again. Again. A teacher in your pocket!

9. **Countdown timer** – set your timer for 15 minutes. Do some revision. Then take a break for 5 minutes. Repeat as necessary.

10. **Send to Kindle** – use this app to send documents to your Kindle to read at your leisure. Also use **Newsstand** to access magazines that may help you widen your knowledge base.

Now think of five more:

1. ....

2. ....

3. ....

4. ....

5. ....

SEE IT! REMEMBER IT!

Do you need to learn the bones of the body?

Simple! Make a skeleton (you'll need card and staples) and then label it. Creating it will help you to remember the way the bones fits together. Or buy one at Halloween – if it's anatomically correct.

Stick it on the back of the toilet door.

When you're flossing, washing and squeezing spots, you'll see the skeleton and, after a while, you'll be getting quite familiar with all those bones.

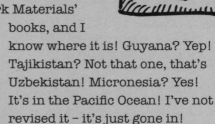

Tim says:

We have a shower curtain at home with a map of the world on it. Since putting it up, my world geography has got so much better. Svalbard? Yep, it's a real place and not just in Philip Pullman's 'His Dark Materials' books, and I know where it is! Guyana? Yep! Tajikistan? Not that one, that's Uzbekistan! Micronesia? Yes! It's in the Pacific Ocean! I've not revised it – it's just gone in!

STICKY NOTES

Write or draw things on sticky notes and then put them where you'll see them. Seeing them day in, day out will help you remember.

DIET
1
2
3
4

Biscuit tin?
Check!

Fridge door?
Check!

Wardrobe door?
Check!

Mirror in your room?
Check!

Dad's massive slap-head?
Best not, eh.

NIGHT NIGHT! GOOD MORNING!

This is a simple 'work smart not hard' technique:

1. Get an index card or a postcard.

2. Draw/write on it what you need to learn.

3. Put it by your bed.

4. Look at it before you go to bed.

5. Look at it when you wake up.

6. When you know it, change the card.

HELPFUL REVISION KIT

* Paper

* Pens

* Coloured pens

* Notepad

* Large sheets of paper (sugar paper or similar)

* Sticky notes

* A diary (with the exams marked in, so you know how long you have until each paper)

* Index cards

* Ring binder, with dividers for each subject (or a ring binder for each subject, with dividers marking out each topic)

It might be helpful to get some study guides for specific subjects too.

How are you going to pay for all these things? Have you got a plan?

MIND YOUR LANGUAGE

Here are some helpful hints for revising for MFL exams and orals.

* Make cue cards to help you learn vocabulary. Get someone to test you regularly.

* Try to learn five words every day in the language you are studying. Be sure of the spelling and pronunciation.

* Label items around the house with vocabulary sticky notes.

* Listen to as much of the target language as you can on TV, radio and in films. Watching foreign language films with subtitles may help. Try watching without the subtitles first. How much can you understand? Can you recognise key phrases or words?

* Buy a newspaper or magazine in the language. Keep a dictionary handy and see how much you can work out.

* Record potential questions and answers on your phone by someone who speaks the target language well. Merge these into a playlist on your MP3 player. Keep listening until you are really familiar.

* Record yourself speaking and listen back to see how you sound. You'll sound weird. Do you keep going with your answer or is there a lot of hesitation? How's your accent?

* Use mnemonics. Try this one for the French verbs which use *être* in the perfect tense: MR V DREAMPANTS (monter, rester, venir, descendre, retourner, entrer, aller, mourir, partir, arriver, naître, tomber, sortir).

* Use online anagram generators to create your own mnemonics.

* Use mind-mapping or spider diagrams for key words and phrases that relate to the same theme. Start with the theme in the middle then branch out with as much relevant material as you can produce. Use lots of small illustrations to reinforce the learning and help the words to stick.

* In your reading exam, always look for cognates (words that look similar to English words). This can really help you to get a handle on what is going on.

* Make sure you know plenty of connectives (e.g. but, especially, whereas, therefore, because – in the target language, obviously!) as these will help to extend your answers into more complex sentences.

* For the listening exam, revise words that show that something either positive or negative follows (e.g. unfortunately, especially). Knowing these words will be useful because, when you hear them, you'll know that an answer is coming.

* In a 'fill the gap with the missing word' exercise, always work out whether you are looking for a noun, verb, adjective or adverb. If you need a noun or adjective, will it be masculine or feminine, singular or plural? If you are looking for a verb, what ending are you looking for? What tense will it be in?

* When writing, check that you have included past, present and future tenses. This will show a greater command of the language.

* Check that you include opinions and reasons in your answers.

* For A2 orals, make sure you know several points on both sides of the argument (e.g. for *and* against racial integration).

EVER-DECREASING CIRCLES

At the start of the revision period, you should have a lot of notes. Loads in fact.

You need to get all that stuff into your head. So, when you've revised a topic, do the following:

1. Get a piece of paper and a dinner plate.

2. Draw round the plate.

3. Write/draw/doodle as many ideas as you can fit into the plate. What's the important stuff? What details are there? Which are the keywords? Use pictures and colour. Highlight and underline important bits. As you go on, you will need to write/draw less. Fewer notes and pictures will be needed to remind you of same amount of detail.

4. Later, get a piece of paper and a small plate.

5. Draw round the plate.

6. Write/draw in the plate circle material from the *same* topic, but this time you have less space. You will draw/write less, but hopefully you will still remember all the original details, which you've not included this time.

7. Later, get a piece of paper and a mug.

8. Draw round the mug.

9. Do the same thing as before – write/draw just enough to fill the mug circle to remind you of the important stuff, but make sure you still know everything you've not written down (but which you included previously).

The circles get smaller. The amount you write gets less. But fewer words are needed to remind you of a lot of detail.

Could you reduce it even further? Could you get everything you need to trigger the memories in a circle drawn round an egg cup?

Get it? Revision is all about triggers. What will trigger your memories?

Try using the three circles opposite to revise what you've learnt from this book already.

HEAR IT! REMEMBER IT!

Some people like to listen to music when they are revising. Others don't.

If you do, why not create the ultimate revision playlist, right here, right now! What would be your top ten tracks?

Write them down. Then make the playlist.

1. ....

2. ....

3. ....

4. ....

5. ....

6. ....

7. ....

8. ....

9. ....

10. ....

Try revising to it now.

Maybe use it on the go too. Create the playlist, but add in some bits of audio revision between tracks (see also idea 5 on page 125).

Just remember: your brain will find it hard to process two things at once, so if you're listening to music when you're trying to remember tricky stuff, it may really hold you back.

Be wise when you revise!

WHERE ARE YOU WORKING?

Let's play word association. If we say 'bed', what is the first thing that comes into your mind?

Most people will think 'sleep' because your bed is not something associated with work.

So, if you do your revision lying on your bed, you aren't really sending the right subconscious messages to your brain.

What *you* are thinking: 'This is a nice comfy place to revise!'

What *your brain* is thinking: 'Ooh! Bed! Time to have a little sleep!'

It won't be long before your eyelids get heavy and you drift off to sleep.

'I must get my head around this really tricky topic … Oooh, but it is a little bit comfy … Zzzzzzzzzzzzz.'

You won't do much revision if you're sleeping! Also, you won't sleep as well at night, and that will lead to more problems.

Big soft sofas with lots of cushions are also a problem for the same reason.

Where should you work?

Find somewhere quiet, away from distractions.

Sit in a chair, ideally with a desk or a table.

Have everything you need to hand, so you don't need to wander off and waste time looking for things. This eats into your revision time.

Have a watch or a clock in sight, so you know when to take breaks.

Don't get sidetracked into doing things that aren't important.

Turn off your phone or put it on silent and move it out of reach.

Focus.

Do some work.

PLANNING YOUR REVISION SESSIONS

Just sitting at a desk, staring at your notes? Try breaking your 15-minute revision slots into activities to keep it moving. Here is how you could use an hour.

Block 1

First 5 minutes: look over what you learnt yesterday (it's always good to come back to something within 24 hours.)

Next 5 minutes: look at something new. Skim read it all first to get an overview, then you can go back and look at it in a bit more detail in the next block of time. Jot down key words/points/images.

Next 3 minutes: memorise what you've written/drawn.

Last 2 minutes: in a revision journal (or notebook), write down three key things from memory that you've learnt.

Take a break.

Block 2

First 5 minutes: look back at what you've learnt in the previous 15 minutes.

Next 8 minutes: test yourself. Do the A–Z test, make a top-ten list of things to remember, draw a diagram from memory, reduce a topic to an image that would fit on the back of a 50p piece, make an MP3 file to listen to later, look at a past paper or use any other strategy we've looked at in this book.

Last 2 minutes: write down three different key points.

Take a break.

Block 3

First 5 minutes: mind map everything you can remember from what you looked at in the first two blocks.

Next 5 minutes: go back to your notes and add to the mind map anything you left off.

Last 5 minutes: from memory, try to draw the mind map again.

You may find the timings here aren't long enough. That's OK – just adjust them accordingly. You may find you need a 20–25 minute block rather than a 15 minute block.

There are lots of different things to do here, though, so don't worry about working for too long – you should be able to concentrate easily.

Plan below how you could break down an hour:

Block 1:

....

....

Block 2:

....

....

Block 3:

....

....

....

....

....

It's not that I'm so smart, it's just that I stay with problems longer.
Albert Einstein

135

NINE USEFUL THINGS TO DO WITH SOCIAL NETWORKING, OR BY GOING ONLINE, TO HELP WITH REVISION

1. Texts. Be accountable. Everyone needs a study buddy. This is the person who checks up on us and makes sure we're working properly. 'Oiy! Have you done any revision today? I have. Get on with it!' Send.

2. Hashtag your revision. If you've learnt something and can condense it into 140 characters, you've got it! Tweet this to others. Set up a hashtag to share revision tips and points (e.g. #StJudesGeogGCSE, #CleeveEnglishALevel).

3. Share helpful videos across your YouTube channel.

4. Skype revision sessions. You're at home, your mate's at home – Skype together as you revise. Test each other.

5. Chatrooms. Stuck? Go and ask someone else.

6. Find past paper questions and send them to friends. Ask them to explain how they would answer, then add to their response.

7. Search for articles in newspapers or magazines – this will give you a greater knowledge of the subject.

8. Go to the revision websites listed in the Appendix.

9. Send each other pictures of your revision notes – maybe on Snapchat.

EISENHOWER MATRIX

This is the Eisenhower matrix (so called because of the quote above by the former US president) – it's a square divided into quadrants, with the information below in each box.

Not urgent and important	Urgent and important
Important goals	Critical activities
Not urgent and not important	Urgent and not important
Distractions	Interruptions

Most activities will fit into one of the boxes above. Let's look at them in turn.

Not urgent and important

These are the things you want to achieve. They are goals you have set for yourself. They may be a particular set of grades.

Your exams are not tomorrow (hopefully) and so, at the moment, they are not an urgent need. They are, however, important. Therefore, it is right that we do *little* and *often*. We chip away at the revision, working towards good knowledge and good skill.

Here's another example: say you want to be an excellent footballer. One aspect of achieving this will be your physical build, but mostly it's to do with training. You train regularly to become good. You don't just do a bit of practice before a game.

Urgent and important

Maybe your exams are tomorrow! They are now urgent and they are still important.

If you haven't done enough work, you will be doing last-minute panic revision. This is not good. There is a place for cramming, but really last-minute cramming should be about *consolidating* your notes and checking you are confident about everything.

In an ideal world, when things become critical (urgent and important) you should be ready and nearly finished. This is about last-minute tweaks and consolidation. This revision is the icing on the cake.

It's the pre-match warm-up and the motivational talk from the coach. It's the sharing of tactics with the team. It's making sure you've remembered your boots.

With course work, it's not about doing it all the night before it's due in, but rather rereading it to make sure it's your best work.

Urgent and not important

Let's imagine you are sitting down to revise and your phone beeps. It's a text from your friend asking you to go out.

Now you are torn. You want to go, but you also need to revise. You ignore it.

Then they text you again.

Then they message you on Facebook and email you.

You look at Twitter and see they've sent you a tweet too.

Then they're ringing you up.

Finally, you hear the doorbell and they're on your doorstep. Arrgghhh!

It's hard to get away these days. New technology means we are always available. There is always someone or something demanding our attention. It interrupts our flow and pulls us off task.

In *Alice's Adventures in Wonderland*, Alice is tempted by a bottle that says 'Drink me'. These days, your PS3 might as well have a note on it saying 'Play me!'

Sometimes we need to resist temptation. Sometimes we need to *prioritise*. We need to say 'no'.

We need to do what is right.

If you don't learn to do this, you will find yourself in the urgent and important box and you won't be prepared.

Remember: if you fail to prepare, you prepare to fail.

Not urgent and not important

Distractions are not always bad. You need to unwind and do things to relax. Hang out with friends … watch rubbish telly … play computer games.

These are all good, and during a stressful year it is important to take time out.

But … if you haven't done your work, you will have a voice in your head telling you that you don't deserve to relax.

This time needs to be *guilt free*. If it isn't, you won't fully relax. Do the work, *then* you can relax without any guilt.

MAKE YOUR OWN CODE

As you work your way through your notes, you'll want to annotate what you've written.

Maybe you'll use a highlighter pen or underline things. You may just add to your existing notes.

It's good to use different colours for this and have specific symbols.

Here are some examples:

K	key point
L	look back through this later
?	I don't get this – ask someone else about it
***	learn this by heart
✓	I know this!

RIGHT PRACTICE

Ebbinghaus Curve of Forgetting

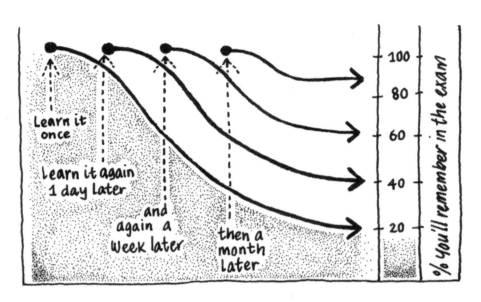

% you'll remember in the exam!

Learn it once

Learn it again 1 day later

and again a week later

then a month later

JUNE

Review your learning after
- a day • a week
- a month • just before the exam & you'll remember most of it!

Psychologist, Hermann Ebbinghaus: 1850-1909

CATS

Here is a way to help you remember some of the main learning points from this chapter:

Creativity – don't just stare at the page. Try to do something a bit creative with your revision: draw a mind map, make some cards or a poster, tweet friends, make an MP3 file of you saying what you need to learn. Use the strategies suggested in this book that work for you. Better still, think of your own.

Attitude – do you think you can do it? If you believe you can, you are more likely to achieve. Hard work and a positive attitude are proven to give students great results in their exams.

What does a poor attitude look like: not believing you are capable? Trying to 'wing it' without any work? Not caring how you do? Assuming everything will be alright and thinking you don't need good grades? Be wise! Get a good attitude.

Time – plan your time. If you fail to plan, you plan to fail.

Break your revision into 15-minute chunks (we concentrate at our best for 15–20 minutes at a time, after which our mind can wander).

Plan to spend a minimum amount of time revising each day. This could be 15 minutes, 30 minutes, an hour or two hours. But once you've decided how much you will do, stick to it.

Create a revision planner (see our two great methods on pages 111–112).

Strengths – play to your strengths and try to work on your weaknesses.

Do you work best straight after school or later in the evening? Are you better first thing in the morning? Do you work better alone or with others? Do you find doodling helps or hinders?

Does it help you to revise online or do you just end up playing games, going on social networking sites and wasting time?

If your Xbox is a massive distraction, unplug it while you are working. We know of one student who took his games console into school and asked his form tutor to lock it away until after the exams!

Work smart not hard.

Use the revision CATS!

Little, but often …

TECHNIQUES THAT (PROBABLY) DON'T WORK

1. Sleeping with your textbook or notes under your pillow! If only this did work ...

2. Placing your faith in your lucky pencil case, studying with your lucky *Star Wars* character or Sylvanian Families figurine on the desk or wearing your lucky pants! You are not on *University Challenge*!

3. Trusting to luck, cosmic benevolence, fate or dubious logic, such as 'I deserve to do well because I looked after gran after she had her fall' or 'I volunteered at the hedgehog sanctuary last summer' (but it's still good to do these things).

4. Wearing glasses to look more intelligent in an attempt to unleash your inner genius. (Note: Wearing someone else's glasses can seriously impair your performance in the exam hall or en route to it.)

5. Hanging around the school brainiacs hoping to absorb some of their knowledge and wisdom in the lunch hall.

6. Growing mad professor hair and wearing a lab coat. All the gear – no idea.

7. Making a wish – 'I wish that I will do well ...'

8. Having a lucky rabbit's foot. Let's face it – it didn't work for the rabbit.

9. Listening to revision in your sleep. The jury is out on this one. Best not risk it.

A PAGE OF REVISION TOP TIPS

* Revision is your job – not your teachers' or your parents' job. Yours! Get on with it!

* The worse you are at a subject, the harder you will need to work. Don't just revise subjects you like.

* Revise as many topics as possible. This will give you more options in the exam.

* The more work you do, the better your results will be.

* Do a lot of practice questions. When you've learnt a subject, try a past paper.

* Don't be afraid to ask for help or for someone to test you.

* If the school is laying on extra revision classes (and they almost certainly are) go along.

* The best time to revise something is just before you are about to forget it! To start with, it may be minutes, then hours, then days, then weeks and months! This is called *spaced repetition*. It works.

* Get some sleep – it is during sleep that your brain processes revision and backs up memories. You need plenty of sleep during your revision time, so the brain can sort out this new information. When we repeat learning, the brain realises it is important information and will send it to our long-term memory during sleep. This is why you can get to the end of the day and think 'I can't remember any of this!' but when you wake up the next day, it's all in there.

* If you can emotionally connect with what you are revising, you are more likely to remember it (think RING – see page 46).

* Don't just read notes over and over. Be active.

* Begin with a subject you don't like and finish with a subject you do like.

SUMMARY

Tick the box if you agree:

☐ Revision is personal – what works for others may not work for you.

☐ You need a plan – create a revision planner.

☐ Work with others.

☐ Revision should be active – see it, hear it, say it, do it!

☐ Take regular breaks.

☐ Get someone to test you.

☐ Teach others.

☐ Images and pictures will help.

☐ Revise in chunks.

☐ Starting is the hardest thing – just do something, however little, just to get going.

☐ Start early.

CHAPTER 5

DEALING WITH EXAMS

THE EXAM ITSELF

These top ten tips are based on advice from teachers who mark exam papers. We've included advice for maths/science-type exams and essay-writing exams. Some papers include both styles (how mean!) so look at both, if necessary.

1. Planning your time before you see the exam paper

The first thing to do is make sure you know the format of the exam. Teachers can help with this as exam formats tend to be consistent year after year. You will probably have done practice exams (mocks). If you've done so many you're sick of them, it probably means you're ready. You should know the best tactics before you even get to your seat.

For example, if the exam is 60 minutes long with 40 questions – starting easy then typically becoming harder, with marks allocated shown for each question up to a total of 60 – you can work out you have one minute per mark. Carefully read over the entire exam paper. Spend up to five minutes reading before you write anything. In this time, work out which questions you are going to answer, which order you are going to answer them in and how much time you are going to spend answering each question.

Take careful note of the marking scheme (see below) when making your plan. Write down the plan on the back sheet of your answer book – you can always cross it out later. This will help you to feel in control, calm and focused.

2. Essay-style questions

Don't be tempted to answer a question on a subject just because it's the one you know most about. It might be a really awkward question. Are you sure you can do it? Which parts can you do? Does it ask for a comparison with another topic you know nothing about? How many marks do you think you could get on the parts of the question you can do? Is there an easier question on a subject you didn't study as much in which you could score more marks? Spending a minute or two selecting the best questions to answer can reap huge benefits by maximising your total marks. Select the questions likely to give you the most marks.

Reading the whole question is also important because many lead you through a problem (e.g. the answer to the first part is used in the second part) or hint at the right way to construct your answer. Make sure you spot any clues in later parts of the question about what the examiner is expecting.

David says:

An examiner recently told me that he often marks answers by students who haven't grasped what the question is asking. They waste time regurgitating information that can only be given zero marks. There is often another question on the paper that could have scored them more marks.

Also common is a long essay on a question that clearly says one mark. Some students write in the margins and in smaller and smaller writing to fit in their response. The amount of space available in a booklet-style exam paper is a big clue to the length of answer required. You are wasting your time twice by writing stuff that will get you no extra marks and depriving yourself of time later on.

Your aim is to get the best mark you can on the whole paper, not just on the question you happen to be doing at the time. Your time plan can be a little flexible, but if you spend more time on one question, try to speed up a little bit later on (whilst avoiding mistakes).

3. Do the easiest questions first

There is no rule to say that you have to answer the questions in the order they are printed in the exam paper. Starting with a couple of questions you understand well at the start of an exam is a perfect confidence boost and can help get you into a flow state for the rest of the exam. When you reach harder questions, take a deep breath and remind yourself you've already built up marks from earlier.

Also, easier questions will take up less of your time than tough questions. That means you'll have more time on the more difficult ones. This prevents the cycle of starting a question and leaving it partway through. This pattern lowers confidence and, ultimately, wastes time as you flip between questions.

This tactic is especially effective if your aim is a grade C, as you will benefit more from tactical question choice. If you're after an A, you'll have to answer all the questions anyway.

4. Look at the marking schemes for clues about the right length of answer

Marking schemes are strict to ensure fairness. So, if there are four marks available for the 'features of a desert' or 'rise of the Nazi Party', then the marking scheme will usually expect four key points from a list of five or six, with one mark for each of them up to a maximum of four.

You can be fairly sure that if you haven't made four key points, you've missed something. Perhaps you could draw an arrow to remind you, so that if you have time later on or an answer flashes into your head, you'll know quickly where to return to fill in a gap. There are often four bullet points on the lines beneath the question, which lets you know how you are expected to answer. Some students still write long answers to questions with just one or two marks. Simply knowing extra stuff won't get you extra marks, so you are better advised to move on to other questions.

Equally, if you get stuck on a question, move on. Staring at a question you don't know how to answer is wasting time. Draw an arrow, or similar, to mark the place so that you can return to it later if you have a flash of inspiration.

5. Take a bottle of water in with you and sip it slowly throughout

Sipping water is a good way of staying calm. Also, some people sweat heavily during exams! There is research which suggests that drinking water can make a significant difference to your grades.

Inside the Brain Box

Research from 2012 by Dr Chris Pawson, from the University of East London, suggests that students who drink water during exams could expect to see their grades improve by up to 5%. The reasons may be psychological, as well as physiological, but the positive impact was significant.

6. Guess for success

Estimate mathematical answers to help you identify obvious errors that you could easily rectify. If your answer for the distance between the Moon and Earth was 3,840 *millimetres* you can be pretty sure you're wrong! Even if you don't have time to go back and correct the mistake, at least write something to indicate that you know it's wrong, as you may be given a mark for your earlier calculations.

7. Always explain what you are doing

In longer questions, especially if you don't arrive at the correct answer, explain what you are doing and show your workings out, even dead ends, as this gives the examiner a chance to give you some, or most, of the marks. In essays, the equivalent is to use bullet points or mind maps to demonstrate knowledge before you run out of time.

8. At the 15-minutes-to-go point, stop and check what you still need to complete

If you've only got time to do one question fully, but have two questions left, what is the best thing to do? The simplest way to maximise your marks is to do the first half of both questions. You gain marks faster at the start of a question than at the end. If you don't have time to write sentences, then write bullet points.

If you are really pressed for time, a mind map showing key points could also secure you some marks. If you don't have time to do calculations, write and explain what calculations you would do. The marker can then give you some marks for method. Obviously, bullet points aren't ideal, so it's best to avoid them if you can, but as a last resort they're better than nothing.

9. Don't leave early

The only possible excuse for leaving early is when you're absolutely sure that you've got 100% – and that is unlikely to happen. There is always *something* you can do to improve your paper. Check, and check again. When you've finished, start from the beginning and try to do the questions in different ways, and check they agree. Add more explanations. Correct spelling mistakes.

10. For maths and science papers be CUTE

Calculations – have you checked calculations? Do answers to different parts of the question agree?

Units – grams, cubic metres, x and y axes, km, mph … Have you included the units you're using? Do the units all make sense and agree?

True – have you answered the question asked, not just spewed out what you know? Have you fully described what you were asked to explain and not omitted something obvious or crucial? Read the question and answer the question – the whole question and nothing but the question, as they say in courtroom dramas.

Examiner's eyes – finally, read through your answers as if you were the examiner. Are they clear? Is what you meant to say what you actually said?

Be CUTE!

Other exam advice

✳ **Write short sentences** – it will make your answers far easier to read and mark. Think about the poor examiners who have to pore over numerous papers. If they can get the facts from you quickly, they will be more on your side.

✳ **Never start an answer with 'Because ...'** – frame answers as proper, stand-alone sentences. This will make your answers stronger.

✳ **Memory dump** – it's good to get key ideas and information down at the start of the paper. Maybe write some key notes or draw a quick mind map. It's good to be in control from the start.

✳ **Avoid getting sucked into an autopsy of the paper straight after you come out** – you may have another exam later in the day. Stay calm. Go back to mentally preparing yourself for the next paper.

KEY THINGS TO DO DURING THE EXAM PERIOD

✳ **Exercise** – get out! Get your heart rate up! Better fitness means more energy and improved concentration.

✳ **Water** – make sure you aren't dehydrated. Plenty of water is good for you.

✳ **Daylight** – you're not a vampire. Go out and get some light!

✳ **Eat healthily** – lay off the junk food. Too much bread can leave some people feeling bloated and tired. Foods high in processed sugar will give you an immediate high but will finish with a crash. Foods that contain natural sugars (e.g. strawberries, bananas) are better because the fibre slows down the digestion of glucose (sugars) so you don't get the high and the low.

✳ **Go to bed** – are you getting at least eight hours sleep? You need to.

✳ **Talk to others** – you're all in it together. Talk to each other about feeling stressed. A problem shared is a problem halved.

✳ **Keep going!** – don't give up. Keep working to the end. Don't quit revision until you've finished your final paper. It's a marathon, not a sprint!

✳ **Never, ever, do drugs!** – yes, we sound like old farts, but it's still very good advice. Never get drunk the night before an exam and don't be drunk or stoned in an exam. Ever.

Inside the Brain Box

Exam time can be stressful, so the University of Aberdeen set up a special 'puppy room' where students could visit the puppies and de-stress!

Following the success of other puppy rooms in Canada and the United States, the university hoped to boost students' health and grades.

So, if you're feeling stressed – go and play with a puppy!

A SANDWICH FOR YOU!

An essay is like a sandwich.

You need two pieces of bread to hold your sandwich together. If they weren't there, all the fillings would mix together and you'd be left with a total mess.

The top piece of bread is your introduction. Hook your reader in and set out where you are going. Keep it short.

The bottom bit of bread is your conclusion. Here, you should be drawing the threads together and rounding off the essay.

The four or five fillings are the meat of your essay. Think about your essay comprising of around four or five paragraphs. Each one should explore a different point. As in a sandwich, the layers of your essay should be distinct.

You may find it helpful to cover these points in each paragraph:

✳ Position: what are you attempting to argue?

✳ Explain: why do you hold this opinion?

✳ Example: facts, figures, statistics and evidence to back up your argument.

✳ Expand: a counter-argument (explain why you don't hold this view).

✳ Point: restate your position and draw the threads of the paragraph together.

Make sure you are answering the question posed. If you include a page of background or description, it may reward you with no points. Stay on task. Don't just tell the story! Try to refer back to the question throughout the essay.

Always support your arguments, theories or findings with evidence. Use your knowledge to back up your answers. Avoid phrases like 'I think …' and instead use 'Evidence suggests …' – and then cite the evidence.

Most marks will be awarded for your skills in thinking for yourself and making your own arguments. In other words, use *analysis* and *evaluation*.

Analysis means exploring different sides of an argument.

Evaluation will involve drawing some conclusions. Offer solutions or alternatives, if appropriate.

A sandwich needs the bread to hold it together. Without it, as we've said, all the fillings would mix together and become a mess. Your essay should be like biting into a sandwich – your teeth pass through the top bit of bread (introduction), then the first filling (point one), then the second (point two), then the third (point three) and so on. Finally, they will chomp through the bottom piece of bread (your conclusion).

In summary

★ **Tell them what you're going to tell them** – introduction. Don't go into too much detail, but highlight the areas you will explore.

★ **Tell them** – the main body of your essay. Three or four main points explored across four or five paragraphs, each one illustrating another point.

★ **Tell them what you've told them** – conclusion. Rounding things off and pulling together your argument. Try to say something new in the conclusion – don't just summarise everything you've written.

SOME ADVICE ABOUT SPEAKING AND LISTENING

Generally, people are more afraid of public speaking than they are of dying! How odd is that? Would you rather be delivering the eulogy or lying in the box?

Consequently, speaking and listening assessments or MFL oral assessments can be hugely nerve-racking. Here are some ideas to help you perform well in these assessments:

* **Keep eye contact** – look the audience or the examiner in the eye. Don't look at the floor or the ceiling. Don't scan – where you just move your eyes left to right and back again. Avoid 'stalker syndrome' – where you just look at one person (unless there is only one person)!

* **Use all the Ps**
    * *Pitch* (high or low) – make sure you aren't speaking in a monotone. Also don't be super squeaky. Nerves will send our pitch upwards – boys tend to end up sounding like girls and girls end up only being audible to dogs!
    * *Pace* (how fast) – nerves make you speed up. Go slow.
    * *Power* (how loud or soft) – make sure you can be heard. If you are nervous, bringing up your volume will make you sound more confident.
    * *Pause* – give yourself some thinking time. It's OK to pause. It allows you time to think and your listener has time to take in and reflect on what you've said.

* **Gesture** – try to speak with your hands. Look animated! Keep your gestures open – don't have your arms folded or your hands in pockets or behind your back.

* **Movement** – if you have room, and are speaking to a crowd, use all the space and don't feel you have to stay in one spot. Try not to wander, though – always move with purpose.

* **Smile!** – even if you feel terrified, a smile will make you look more confident.

- ✳ **Posture** – stand tall or sit up straight. Keep your feet shoulder-width apart and try not to cross your legs.

- ✳ **Sound enthusiastic** – this makes a world of difference. If you sound bored, your audience will get bored too. If you speak with passion, everyone will listen.

- ✳ **Ask rhetorical questions** – it will keep your audience thinking.

- ✳ **Use quotes or stories** – human interest really helps to engage the crowd.

- ✳ **Plan** – always have a good idea about what you want to talk about and practice in advance.

BOARD GAMES

No, not like Monopoly or Cluedo – as in *exam* boards.

There are loads of them – and they all focus on different stuff. Some will concentrate on one area of the curriculum, while others won't touch it.

You need to know which board you are studying. Often, the revision guides you can buy will cover different material from the exam board producing your exam. Make sure you know which one is setting your paper. Your teachers will be able to tell you.

You can then look at the syllabus and past papers on their websites (these are listed in the Appendix).

DESCRIBE, EXPLAIN, DISCUSS AND COMPARE

Let's think about what the examiners want in model answers. This can be summed up as describe, explain, discuss and compare.

So, what is the difference?

Here is a tin of beans.

First up, *describe* the beans:

> Beans are small pulses served in tomato sauce. They come in a metal can, with a paper label. The beans are baked, but require heating.

Next, *explain* the beans:

> Beans are an easy-to-prepare food. They can be served as a complement or on toast as a simple meal. They are high in fibre and are said to be healthy.

Then, *discuss* the beans:

> Some people like beans because of their health benefits and because of their ease of preparation. Other people dislike the taste and find they make them flatulent. It could be argued that low-salt beans are a better alternative, because they can be substituted for normal beans as a more heart-friendly product. On the other hand, despite the health benefits, many feel low-salt beans are lacking in taste. There are many different producers of tinned baked beans, with chains of supermarkets producing cheaper products, often including a 'basics' or 'value' version. Connoisseurs would argue that these often have an inferior taste to high-end branded products and that the sauce is 'watery'. However, if you are living on a low income, for example a student, this might be a better option.

Here is a tin of spaghetti.

Finally, *compare* and *contrast* beans and spaghetti:

> Beans and spaghetti are sold in similar tins with similar labels. They are both served in tomato sauce. They are both convenience foods and can be served in similar ways, for example on toast.

> However, a bean is a pulse and spaghetti is a pasta product. Beans are small and round whilst spaghetti is long and thin. Beans are a good source of protein, whereas spaghetti is made from wheat and is a source of carbohydrate.

Get the difference?

Describing is about listing the *features*.

Explaining is about *uses* and *benefits*.

Discussion is about arguments – the *pros* and *cons*.

Compare and contrast is about *similarities* and *differences*.

Now you try:

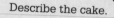

Describe the cake.

Explain the cake.

Discuss the cake.

Now compare cake and biscuits.

Alternatively, think about Play Station and Xbox. Could you describe, explain, discuss and compare and contrast these two platforms?

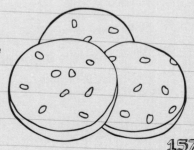

A PAGE OF TOP TIPS FOR EXAMS

✹ Try not to talk to people before going in – if they start yammering about how much they know, it might wobble you.

✹ Go for a little walk.

✹ Practise calm breathing.

✹ Have a digital detox – avoid going online before the exam. Avoid TV too.

✹ Listen to some calming music.

✹ Go to the loo before you enter the room.

✹ Have something to eat an hour or two before the exam. Bananas are good for energy.

✹ Make sure your calculator has batteries in it.

✹ It's OK to be a bit nervous. Try to relax – deep breathing is good. If you have a mantra to repeat, do it now: 'I'm OK … I've learnt this …' Stretch. Do relaxation exercises.

✹ Pray! No one can prove the existence of God, but there has been some conclusive research into the effect that prayer can have on an individual's state of mind! And if there is a God – it might just help …

✹ Don't try to cheat – don't write things on your arms or try to smuggle in a phone.

✹ Take sweets into the exam (but read what we've said about sugar highs).

✹ If the question requires you to look at data (e.g. a graph or map), all the information to get a good mark is on the page. Take advantage of easy marks.

✹ Plan your time – if a paper is made up of three essays, make sure you split the time evenly.

✹ Make notes for an essay, loosely plan the structure and then write it.

✹ You don't need to answer the questions in order.

✹ Don't wear ill-fitting clothes. Make sure you aren't going to be too hot or too cold.

- If you have a wobbly desk, let the invigilator know – but do it at the start.

- Reread your answers and make sure you've not written something really stupid. Check grammar and spelling. Keep your work neat, including your handwriting. Don't worry if your writing is a little messy – just make sure it can be read!

- Show your workings. If you run out of time, use notes – you may still get marks for your ideas.

- If the invigilator pacing up and down is annoying you, tell them. They do need to check things, but if you are being thrown by their behaviour, it's good to make them aware.

TOP TEN THINGS TO DO IN EXAMS

1. Read the questions properly. And look at the back of the paper – there may be a load more questions there that you haven't seen!

2. Reread each question. Understand what is being asked of you. Don't spend ages describing something if you've been asked to explain or discuss it.

3. Have a bottle of water with you.

4. Make sure you have the right equipment – that your pens work, your pencils aren't broken and so on.

5. Have a good night's sleep before the exam.

6. Do the easy questions first.

7. Read how many marks each question is worth – don't spend 10 minutes on a question worth 3 points. Don't spend 3 minutes on a question worth 20 points.

8. Don't panic! But do keep an eye on the clock.

9. Check your answers.

10. Don't leave any gaps – if you don't know, guess!

TOP TEN THINGS NOT TO DO IN EXAMS

1. Sing.

2. Fall asleep.

3. Try to look at other people's work.

4. Get an uncontrollable fit of the giggles.

5. Write on the table.

6. Put chewing gum under the seat. Or in your hair. Or in someone else's hair.

7. Answer a phone call.

8. Try to throw balls of paper into the bin from ten metres. You're not Michael Jordan.

9. Release solids, liquids or gases from your body. Eugh!

10. By this point, it's too late. Just do your best. Answer the questions you do know how to answer, and guess the rest!

SUMMARY

Tick the box if you agree:

☐ Get plenty of sleep the night before the exam.

☐ Read the paper properly.

☐ Try to keep calm: avoid people you know will stress you out.

☐ Make sure you understand what the examiner is asking of you.

☐ If you run out of time, make notes or bullet points.

☐ Do the easiest questions first to boost your confidence.

☐ Don't turn up hungry or thirsty.

☐ Try your best.

☐ Don't give up.

CHAPTER 6

DEALING WITH RESULTS

THE RESULTS ARE OUT, WHAT NOW?

Note: Look at this section long before your results are out. It is best to prepare yourself for the next step well in advance.

If you know what to do following a 'best case' or 'worst case' scenario, you will minimise stress later on.

Me (if I do really well)

Me (if I don't do well)

My destination (first-choice course/career): ....

....

List a few other options (my back-up plans):

....

....

....

Check these plans with the course providers.

Make a list of the people who you will turn to after you receive your results (include their contact details):

1. ....

2. ....

3. ....

If your results were on target, you should be able to enjoy a break and prepare for the next stage of your education or getting a job.

If you didn't achieve the results you needed (some people do much better than they thought or much worse than they'd hoped for), then you may need to look at an alternative plan.

This is not a time to panic. It is a time to rationally assess your options.

Before reassessing your life, check with your teachers that they are not recommending you query your results. You do have choices and it is important to consider all of the alternatives before making a rash decision you may later regret.

Write down on a piece of paper what choices you think you have. Seek information and advice from as many sources as possible about any further options available. Don't try to pick a best option just yet – it is important to identify all the possibilities first.

Hopefully, the information you gather will not be contradictory. If it is, further research will be needed. Impartial advice is best, but it's OK to gather information from partial sources so long as you know that they may be bigging up their course, training or job.

Finally, create a list of your options (aim for at least three but no more than six). Chunking can help you here.

....

....

....

....

....

....

AFTER YOUR GCSE RESULTS

You've got your results! Well done.

At 16, your best option is probably further full-time study (50% of students go on to do A levels). Of the rest, 35% do a vocational course, 10% an apprenticeship and 5% get a job.

Seek confirmation of your school or college place. Did you get the required grades?

If your results were similar to your predicted grades, usually the institution will be pleased to offer you a place on the course or subject(s) you originally applied for. If they were much better or worse, they may offer you alternative courses. If possible, discuss this during the application process and find out what alternative courses the school/college could offer.

Would you rather stay on at school or go to an FE college? Consider whether the place where you study is more important than the course itself. Does the institution meet your needs? If not, then you should be exploring alternatives well before results day.

Apprenticeships are highly sought after and nearly always oversubscribed, with over ten young people applying for each apprenticeship. What are you doing to make sure that you are selected? Have you organised some work experience (not just that week in Year 10 that the school arranged)? Have you got the best grades possible?

If you've got the right results and your place is sorted, sit back, relax and enjoy the rest of the holiday.

AFTER YOUR A LEVEL/ DIPLOMA RESULTS

At 18, your options are probably full-time study. If you have applied for a university place, you are already within the UCAS system. Make sure you are around when the results come out as you may need to take action. Delay your holiday to Magaluf by a few days if possible!

If your results are worse than predicted/required for your conditional firm offer, you need to find out whether or not you are still being offered the place, either directly with the university or through UCAS Track.

For a small number of people, a priority re-mark can be the right option, especially if the university is willing to hold your place. Check with the teachers who know you well before setting off on this route. There will be a cost for this too and your school or college can advise you. You might even be able to haggle on cost! The re-mark can usually be done within 72 hours. Ofqual offer more information – visit: www2.ofqual.gov.uk/help-and-support/94-articles/162-exams-doctor or email: examsdoctor@ofqual.gov.uk.

If you aren't offered your conditional firm (CF) or conditional insurance (CI) place, you will automatically enter UCAS Clearing. In 2012, nearly 12,000 places weren't filled when the results came out, so stay positive!

Conversely, if your results were far better than your predicted grades and you would like to reconsider your course choice, you can contact universities and ask if they have places in UCAS Adjustment.

All course vacancies are advertised online and you can contact universities and attempt to secure a place. This can be a tense time for both students and university staff, so be polite and patient when you speak to people. Stay calm and only enquire and accept a place on a course that you *really* want to commit to for three years of your life.

Think long and hard about retakes. These can only be done in the following year, so you will need to wait another nine months before you can resit the paper. Is it worth it? This is really only a route to go down if you need specific grades to get onto a certain course at a certain university. Do you have what it takes to redo the year when many of your friends will be moving on?

If you are going to do retakes, remember that universities will want to know that you're doing something productive with the year out. Don't expect to idle it away, waiting for the exams the following summer.

The gap year option appeals to some students who combine work and travel for a year, whilst reapplying through UCAS in the next cycle. The advantage of applying once you have your results is that you have your grades upfront and there is no uncertainty.

Grades and points and what they mean (%)

	A	B	C	D	E
AS	60	50	40	30	20
A2	260	100	80	60	40

Qualification levels

	Level	Description
E	Entry	Basic qualifications related to straightforward work tasks, such as food hygiene or data input.
1	Beginner	Further qualifications linked to job tasks. Usually studied after school in a college or work setting.
2	Intermediate	Broader qualifications at a similar level to GCSEs. These courses generally last an academic year.
3	Advanced	Broad or specific qualifications such as A levels or Advanced Diplomas. Usually studied after Year 11 in school sixth forms, colleges or as part of some apprenticeships. Often referred to as further education. Usually last two academic years.
4	Higher education	Degree course level study. Usually take three academic years to complete.
5	Post-graduate	Professional qualifications allowing someone to practice a profession (e.g. accountant, lawyer, doctor, architect, surveyor, teacher).

165

Of course, not everyone applies to university and there are jobs and apprenticeships available to students leaving further education.

If you can answer all these questions *before* applying to university, then you're ready to apply!

* What are my alternatives to university?
* Do I want to live at home or move away?
* What grades/points are required?
* What reputation does the university have for my subject?
* What are the facilities like for my subject?
* What happens to graduates at the university studying the course?
* Will the course help me get the job I want?
* Will I get accommodation in my first year?
* Will I have to cook my own meals in my first year?
* Does the university have a good nightlife?
* Does the university cater for my sports/hobbies/interests?
* Is it a campus university?
* Do I want to live in a large city?
* Will I get the opportunity to go abroad as part of the course?
* Is it a sandwich course?
* How will I be assessed (e.g. continuous assessment, course/module exams)?
* How much will the fees cost me and what financial support (including bursaries) is available?
* How much will my accommodation cost?
* What do my peers think of my plans?
* What do my parents/teachers think of my plans?

Top tips for getting into university

1. Have a passion for your subject – do you *really* want to study this subject?

2. Show commitment – gain work experience in the field you wish to study.

3. Find out about the course you're applying for – what do you like about it? What are the differences between the courses each university offers?

4. Talk to others who've studied this subject – what are their experiences?

5. Be realistic – if the requirement is three As and you're heading for two Ds and an E, this may not be the course for you!

6. Do what *you* want to do (not what your parents or teachers expect you to do)?

7. Prepare for the interview. Find out how the interview will be conducted and think about potential answers for the type of questions you may be asked.

8. Get good grades at A level.

9. Consider doing an extended study project.

10. Ask yourself, 'Why do I want to do that subject at *that* particular institution?' Have an answer.

FINAL THOUGHTS

We're nearly at the end now! (Aaaah.)

Hopefully you've found that your time in *The Brain Box* has been helpful. Learning is for life, not just school or college, so you may feel the need to revisit *The Brain Box* in years to come. Tuck it away safely. Call on it when you need it ...

As we said at the start, we can't tell you how to do all these things – we can only advise. We don't take responsibility for your success (or failure), but please do weigh our advice and make up your own mind. If you think it's helped, then that's great! If you don't – well, we were trying our best. In the end, it's all any of us can do.

So, before we go, a final activity from David.

Success is a combination of what we know and what we do with what we know.

Give yourself a score from 1 to 10 based on what you currently know about a topic, and a score from 1 to 10 based on how effectively you currently use and apply what you know. Then multiply the two numbers together and determine your current performance level as a percentage.

Converting the two numbers to a percentage usually makes our current score seem low. This reflects the adage, 'the sum is greater than its parts'. In learning and revision, we need to pay attention to all the areas covered in this book. Falling down in one section can bring your overall performance right down.

For example, what is your score on making a bed?

You may feel, on a scale of 1 to 10, that you are about an 8 with regard to bed-making. You know most of the basics, but there may be some mysteries about the art of bed-making about which you know nothing at all (such as 'hospital corners' or 'turning down').

However, you may rarely make your bed, so this knowledge isn't very helpful! So you would score yourself around a 2 for use and application.

Your score would be as follows:

8 (knowledge) x 2 (use and application) = 16%

You can use the formula in many areas of life but let's use study skills this one last time.

What do you know about study skills and how are you using them?

(a) Current knowledge: _____ out of 10

(b) Current use of this knowledge: _____ out of 10

Multiply both numbers (a x b): _____%

What can you do to improve your score?

What do you think about your current score?

David says:

One of my favourite pieces of research involves fish.

Scientists studied the predatory pike. First they placed a pike in a tank full of tasty minnows. The pike quickly ate all the minnows.

Next, they placed more minnows in an upturned glass bowl inside the tank. The pike soon learned it could not reach the minnows.

Then the scientists removed the bowl, but the pike retained its learned behaviour. It would not attempt to eat the minnows and they swam freely around the tank.

What people believe is often fixed and holds them back as the world around them changes.

We believe we can be and do far more than we think we can. We would be delighted if you use some of the ideas from this book to help you believe and achieve more of your potential.

Tim says:

When I was a teenager, my mum gave me a small card inscribed with the words of the poem 'If' by Rudyard Kipling (of *The Jungle Book*'s fame).

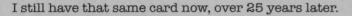

I still have that same card now, over 25 years later.

It's a great poem. If you've never read it, you really should. In it, Kipling gives advice to his son about his future life as an adult. It explores many of the characteristics and skills we have discussed in this book.

Below is an adaptation of the poem for the contemporary world.

Which of the traits have you developed so far? You may like to tick them off.

These are Kipling's ideas of what it means to be an adult. What are yours? Are you getting there? It takes a while. But you will.

If ...

Can you keep your cool when everyone else is freaking out, and blaming you for stuff that really isn't your fault?

Can you still believe in yourself when other people don't believe in you at all, whilst not holding their lack of faith in you against them (like you, they are only human)?

Have you the patience to wait for things, but not get fed up of waiting and become demoralised and impatient?

Can you cope when people tell lies about you, without resorting to telling lies about other people?

When people say they hate you or say hateful stuff about you, have you the strength of character not to become a hater too?

Can you keep the moral high ground but not look like a big-head or a know-it-all?

Can you dare to dream big dreams, but not lose your grip on reality and the here and now?

Can you think for yourself but not over-think things so you end up self-obsessed or too stressed out?

Can you experience success and not let it go to your head, or suffer failure but not give up or get depressed?

Can you cope when people misquote you for their own purposes and your reputation gets dragged through the mud?

Could you handle it if you worked amazingly hard for something – blood, sweat and tears – only to lose it all? Could you then start all over again?

Can you make a foolish mistake, as we all do, but learn from it?

Are you good with money? Have you learnt the value of it?

Can you keep going when you are worn out?

When your body, mind and brain are telling you to quit, can you find the strength to keep going and believe things will eventually turn a corner and get better?

Can you be with your peers, get on with everyone, but still be your own person and not give in to peer pressure?

Can you mix with lots of different people from all walks of life – from royalty to the people in the street?

Can you keep your chin up even when people let you down – whether friends or enemies (and they will)?

Can you be relied on, but not walked over and taken advantage of?

Can you fill each moment of your life with something worthwhile?

If you can, you'll be as near to an adult as any of us get ...

You'll be a Brain Box!

Congratulations!

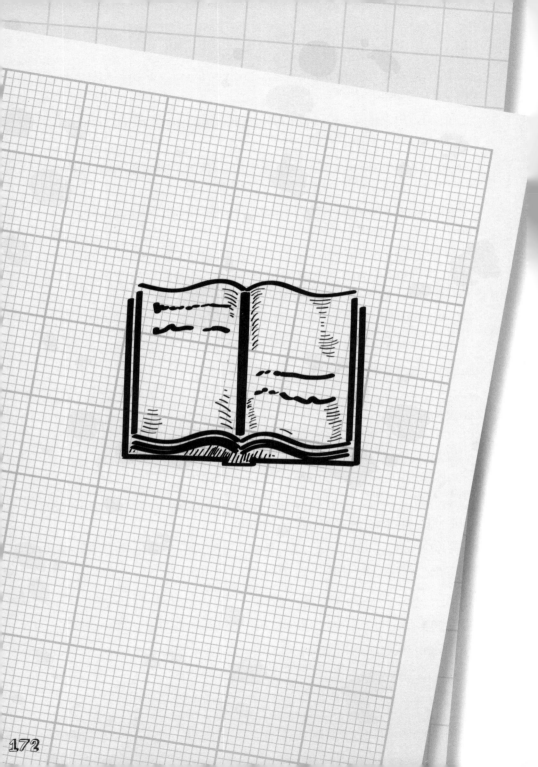

TEARS, TANTRUMS AND TIREDNESS

This section offers some advice for parents, so give this to them – or better still, ask them to buy their own copy of the book!

Hi Mum, Dad, Uncle, Auntie, carer, social worker, brother, sister, weird family friend who everyone calls 'Uncle' but isn't really any relative at all … Welcome to *The Brain Box*!

We're guessing you're reading this because the owner of the book is about to sit some serious exams. You want them to do well, right?

Good. So, it's important to support them in the correct way. The bad news is, they are teenagers, and teenagers tend to make bad choices. It's not their fault – they are still a work in progress. Making the wrong choices is part of the process we all go through, as teens, to help us learn how to make the right choices. So nagging them and giving them a tough ride isn't always the best route. They will just resent you and probably do even less work as a result (if that's even possible!).

So, what can you do? Well, here is our idiot's guide/checklist to supporting a teen through their exams.

✳ **Stay calm!** Shouting at them and losing your temper is usually counterproductive. Encouragement is always the best approach.

Confrontational: 'You haven't done any work! Go and revise! NOW! Or I'll take your phone away and throw it in the bin.'

Encouraging: 'Would it help if I tested you later on what you've learnt? I can do that at about 9 p.m., so you've got about an hour to do your revision. Then we can all watch that programme you want to watch.' It may not work, but reasoned argument is better than shouting.

CUT OUT

Rewards are good! You need to set rewards and stick to them. Long-term (i.e. results-driven – 'Get 10 As and you can go to Newquay with your mates') rewards are good, but short-term is better as your average teen finds it easier to live in the moment ('You can be excused from washing up tonight if you do an hour of revision before dinner'). If they don't uphold their end of the bargain, don't uphold yours. If you give them their reward, and they haven't deserved it, they will never do what they need to do.

Shhh. They need some peace and quiet to work. Is the atmosphere in the house helpful? If there are younger, noisier siblings, they need to understand that big brother/sister needs some space. And no loud arguments in the house please: a war zone is not a work zone.

Invite their friends around. One big theme in this book is the need to work with others. Revision doesn't have to be a solitary act. Encourage them to invite their friends around to revise as a pair or group. Try not to embarrass them (old photos of them as a child may be sweet to you, but will be torture for them).

Space is important. In their room or at the table, give them space to work. Revising on their bed is not a good place to learn. Bed is for sleep. Revision is boring. Revision + bed = sleep. Sleep = no work.

They need to take regular breaks. Twenty minutes is fine for each 'block' of revision. They should take short (5–10 minute) breaks between each block.

Revision needs focus. They will tell you that they can multitask by revising, watching TV, playing the Xbox, texting and listening to music, all at the same time. They can't. You probably paid for these things, so you have a right to take them away.

They may work better with music playing. We are all different. Some people find it helps, others find it a distraction. Of course, what they are listening to will make a big difference. Thrash metal is never good for concentration! Ever. Remember: they can only truly concentrate on one thing properly at a time. But music may make it more palatable.

Company is good. They don't need to be on their own to work (see 'Invite their friends around'). Some individuals just find it easier to concentrate when there are other people in the room. The energy of others busying themselves keeps them alert.

You can test them. Or be on hand to have them explain things to you. It's one of the best ways to learn.

CUT OUT

The world won't end if they don't get the grades they should. It will be bad, it will not be a positive outcome, but life will go on and they will find their way. Too much pressure will make some students buckle. Reinforce that it is important for them to do well, to do their best, but that you will still love them whatever happens.

The school is your friend. They want your child to do well too, and will happily supply advice, information and support as needed. Communicate with them. Stay calm and trust them – they are the experts. But don't be afraid to share your fears. Always stay calm and respectful. Shouting at teachers doesn't achieve anything, just as teachers shouting at students rarely achieves anything either! Sometimes schools don't get it right though, through no fault of their own – they are large and have many students – so it is important to speak up if something seems amiss. But do it in a constructive way.

Online is fine. Not everything on the Internet is designed to ensnare, distract or subvert – your child can also gain much-needed support. Here are some useful sites:

> www.getrevising.co.uk
>
> www.bbc.co.uk/schools/revision
>
> www.s-cool.co.uk

The school may have online learning available for them too or may have subscribed to certain sites (e.g. www.samlearning.com).

The exam board websites also have past papers and the syllabuses for each subject. The school can tell you which board the students are sitting. The websites are listed in the Appendix.

Subject-specific revision guides can be helpful but make sure they are for the correct exam board.

They need their sleep. Roughly eight hours of it, every night. A curfew on technology isn't a bad idea. Turn off the Internet router at 9.30 p.m. Make sure the TV is off by 10 p.m. If they won't be self-disciplined, you may have to have a discussion regarding the removal of the TV from their room (if they have one). Be brave. Be strong.

Give them a day off. If God needed a day off, we do too! If they've revised for six days, it's good for them to take a break for one day. They will be more productive when they come back to it fresh.

CUT OUT

Don't be demanding. Are you placing too many other demands on them? 'We need to go out tonight', 'You need to see your nan', 'You haven't done your chores' – all of these things are important, and routine is good, but make sure they have enough time to do their revision. That is the priority during this time.

Downtime is important. Just because the exams are coming up, it doesn't mean they need to abandon all of their hobbies and interests. It will do them good to have time out to do these things. Ultimately, it will make them more rounded too. Exam results are a rung up to the next stage, but they aren't everything. The skills, thinking, socialisation and so on that come from non-school activities are ultimately as, if not more, important. Keep it in perspective. The time management skills they will learn through balancing these priorities will equip them handsomely for life beyond school.

Working smart not hard is good. Let them put information up on the walls, fridge door, bathroom mirror and so on with facts they need to learn. This will help to slow-drip information into their brains. You will probably end up learning it too!

A good breakfast is important. The following do not constitute a good breakfast: Snickers, Haribo, Red Bull and other energy drinks, donuts, cigarettes, burgers, Skittles, cola or chocolate. Eating well is important. A lot of heavy stodgy food isn't great for concentration. Equally, they will find it hard to concentrate if they are hungry. Encourage them to drink plenty of water and keep fresh fruit in the house. They may not know what fruit is. Tell them.

Keep loving them, whatever. At times they will be vile. They will spurn your help, scream at you, make your life miserable and make you wish you'd never had kids. It is a phase. It will pass. Love them at these times, more than ever. They need to know you are on their side. Encourage them. Love them.

Remember: the darkest hour is just before the dawn.

CUT OUT

APPENDIX

USEFUL WEBSITES

For getting on the right college course:

* www.prospects.ac.uk
* www.ukcoursefinder.com
* www.whatuni.com
* www.thestudentroom.co.uk
* www.push.co.uk
* http://coursefinder.telegraph.co.uk/ – this is like a dating website but will match you to a degree course after asking you some key questions.

For employment options:

These sites are run by students and for students.

* www.nationalcareersservice.direct.gov.uk
* www.icould.com

When looking for work:

* www.jobvacancies.org
* www.gov.uk/jobs-jobsearch
* www.fish4jobs.co.uk
* www.3wjobs.co.uk
* www.jobsite.co.uk
* www.sector1.net
* www.e4s.co.uk

Other useful websites when looking for work:

* www.businesslink.co.uk – support for starting up in business

* www.shell-livewire.org – supporting those who have ideas for self-employment

* www.gapyear.com

* www.apprenticeships.org.uk

For revision:

* www.bbc.co.uk/bitesize

* http://getrevising.co.uk/

* www.s-cool.co.uk

* http://revisionworld.co.uk/

Exam boards. You can find past papers and syllabuses here:

* **AQA:** www.aqa.org.uk

* **Edexcel:** www.edexcel.com

* **OCR:** www.ocr.org.uk

* **Welsh Joint Education Committee:** www.wjec.co.uk

* **Scottish Qualifications Authority:** www.sqa.org.uk

Websites to help with MFL:

* www.spellmaster.com – lots of interactive games

* www.textivate.com – paste up to 500 words of text and get 26 different exercises based on it, such as fill the gaps and reordering tasks

* www.cueprompter.com – an online teleprompter which is helpful for learning chunks of text. This one is great for preparing for oral assessments

* www.linguascope.com – more interactive games

Organisations that offer emotional support:

Childline:

0800 1111

www.childline.org.uk

The Samaritans:

08457 909090

Welsh language line: 0300 123 3011

www.samaritans.org

Get Connected:

0808 808 4994

www.getconnected.org.uk

Jot down any other useful websites here:

ACKNOWLEDGEMENTS

There are numerous people who have supported, encouraged and inspired me on my journey with *The Brain Box* – hopefully I won't miss anyone out. I'd like to thank my co-author, David, who approached me about doing this in the first place and believed I was capable. It was so helpful to work alongside someone who had done it all before and David was a calm and motivating writing partner. Thanks to Caroline and Ian and Bev and all at Crown House for their belief in the idea and taking the risk. Thank you to the designers and illustrators who have done such a sterling job of bringing our ideas to life here on the page.

Our Independent Thinking family are always a huge support and big thanks to Roy, Dave, Hywel, Jim, Simon, Dr Curran and Ian particularly for your ideas and inspiration.

There are many teachers who have continued to place their trust and belief in me to whom I am extremely thankful, so huge thanks to Lois and Maria at St Mary's Chesterfield, Ben Slatter, Kate Pope, Nikki Edwards and many, many others at Cleeve School, Steve Brady, Rob Warren, Ruth Digby, Debi Howell, Derek Pitt, Taranvir Singh Guron at The Achievers' Programme India, Kate Shattock and Linda McQuone. Thank you.

Also, I'd like to thank the many students who took to Twitter after one of my revision sessions to say how much it helped them. I'm glad, and hopefully our book will help many more.

On a personal note, thanks to Libby and Jeremy Wall, not only for some top MFL revision tips, but also for general support and 'being there'. The same goes to The Firkins. Thanks to my Trinity Cheltenham small group of pals, past and present, who have been there for me throughout and have been so encouraging about this project. Thanks, as ever, to Bob – an excellent sounding board and brilliant friend. Thanks to all my family; Bentons and Wigmores alike – all so supportive. I was blessed with parents who were a rock through my exams – without them, there would be no book and little else. I will always be grateful. Finally, I must thank the wife, Clare, who has been with me throughout the creation of this book and who is just amazing.

Thank you all.

Tim Benton

I would like to echo the comments made by Tim and thank all of the people who have helped make this book possible including teachers Lucie Golton and David Sayers for sharing their revision tips. We are motivated to support students, teachers and parents. We hope this book will help students reach their full potential in school and beyond.

David Hodgson

A place for notes …

A place for notes …

A place for notes ...

A place for notes …

A place for notes …